City of Allegory: Book II

The Handy-man's Fix

City of Allegory: Book II

The Handy-man's Fix

A Novel by Brady Goodwin, Jr.

Self-Published through UrbanRemixProject.com

City of Allegory: The Handy-man's Fix

Copyright © 2013, 2015 Brady Goodwin, Jr.

Self-Published by Brady Goodwin through Urbanremixproject.com

Philadelphia, PA

All rights reserved. No part of this publication may be reproduced or transmitted in any form by any means, electronic, mechanical, photocopy, or otherwise, without the prior permission of the publisher.

Printed in the United States of America by Createspace

Cover design by Jemel Rashad

ISBN-10: 098841550X
ISBN-13: 978-0-9884155-0-8

Contents

Prelude: Around the Unending Table 1
Episode 1: Something I Ate 13
An Interlude: Back Around the Table 29
Episode 2: What Needs Fixing 31
Episode Three: Mr. Nice Guy? 49
Episode Four: Electrik-Blue 75
Episode Five: Turn and Run 103
Episode Six: Innocence Lost 127
Episode Seven: Behind the Dark, Red Door 163
Episode Eight: Buried Treasure 193
Episode Nine: Drawing Straw 229
Episode Ten: Under Arrest 261
Episode Eleven: A Beautiful Noise 299
Epilogue: Arrival of the Watchers 313

To Father-figures, Future-fathers & Daughters of all ages.

Prelude

Around the Unending Table

"Please! Please!" she screamed; her voice full of agony. 'Could it really be her?' he wondered. He had never felt pain in this place before, but now it tortured him to hear her voice after all these years, and especially to hear it coming from the bowels of that great pit which was once a great hill. "Please!" the voice continued to rise, "Just bring a drop of that water from the Crystal Sea and let it drip down to me. It's so hot down here; can't you bring me some relief?"

The air was thin where he was. This made it difficult to breathe. But he still went further, closer to the edge in order to see for himself. He looked down at her or, at least, at the familiar face which should have been hers. But he knew not to trust the shape-shifting soul who was slowly but surely scaling his way up out of that pit. He shook his head 'no' as the familiar face transformed into an evil, grotesque smile; a smile that was just as familiar to him as her face. "I better get back to the table," he thought to himself.

Come to think of it, how had he gotten so far away from the feast? So far from Emmanuel? This was not the first time he had gone out on his own. He was always volunteering for some odd job; some service he could render. In fact, his hands were almost always the first in the air whenever volunteers were needed. Back when the city was Nameless, he was used to only fixing things halfway. But now, in Emmanuel City, he looked for and seized every opportunity to use 100 percent of his abilities wherever he could.

However, this was the first time he had ever gone out this far. He ran back through the city and drew comfort from seeing how everything around him was being made new. He even passed those old lions but knew that he had no reason to fear them. They had no interest in him since he was accompanied by that powerful Aroma which sickened them and caused them to lose their appetite.

Around the Unending Table 3

He made it back to the center of the city and found his place at the unending table. There he sat, catching his breath and fighting back tears as he tried to forget what he saw and heard coming from the great pit. He was comforted by a woman who sat near him while they waited for the next dish and the next dissertation from the one who sat at the head of his table.

And what an odd table it was. It seemed to grow right out of the ground, even though it had clearly been implanted there on the day that Emmanuel returned to the city. The table was, in fact, a tree's trunk. But where was the rest of the tree? No matter. Wherever it was now, one thing was clear: this tree was of no ordinary species. Its breadth and width were extraordinary to behold.

But, more odd than the table's shape was the seating arrangement it allowed for, where each guest felt as if he or she was sitting directly in front of the honored Host. This was made possible because, along with the purest oxygen, the partial tree also exhaled a most remarkable element which refracted the city's light. As a result, everyone's sight was constantly being redirected straight to the head of the table where, there sat Emmanuel, whom they called "E-man" for short. These airwaves did not only make him visible to all but, also, audible so that each of his guests could clearly hear his many gracious words which seemed to season the incredible meals which grew, amazingly, right out of the smoothly sanded, wooden table-top.

Granted, it was not just the Living Table that amazed here. All of nature seemed to be supernatural in this new city as it bent and bowed before Emmanuel's eminence. For instance, when Emmanuel spoke—he masterfully manipulated thunder roll and lightning flash to serve as punctuation and exclamation marks for his excellent self-expression. And, whenever a course of the meal was completed, a cool, moist wind would wash over the guests to clear the table and cleanse or purify their hands and hearts—it was as if it was very gently raining sideways and, inside ways.

When Emmanuel was silent, the food was still good. But when he seasoned the savory selections with his speech, the food went from being good to something else; something indescribable that only the soul can define, and that, not with words. Or, should I say, not with any of the words that have been taught to us yet; for we who are still in this world have yet to sit at this bountiful table.

But, if you could join them there, you would quickly come to understand the one and only problem facing the inhabitants of Emmanuel's city—to be precise—the problem of why being called away from that table to serve elsewhere in the city was such an honor, and yet, such a difficult honor to receive. This was because no one in the city wanted to do anything or be anywhere that would take them out of Emmanuel's immediate view. Nor did they want to miss out on hearing his weighty words which always flavored the finest of foods.

For, you see, even though his presence could be sensed everywhere in the city (as he was now shining everywhere that the sun used to shine), still, very few people had yet seen Emmanuel's face. This was because the light which did emanate from him was of the highest degree, so that it hid him from the sight of those who had not been looking at him long enough for their eyes to adjust. And it seemed that just as an individual was getting close to being able to gaze upon Emmanuel's glorious countenance, that individual would be called away from the table to go into the city to serve in some way. There was much work to be done in Emmanuel City and it was an extreme honor for anyone who was called to serve E-man by helping to rebuild his regained realm.

There were quite a few people who tried to remain at the Living Table even though they had been called away from it. So, to ensure participation in the rebuilding process, E-man consulted with his father and passed a law stating that anyone who is not willing to work will not be allowed to eat at his table. Some people went as far as to claim that they were willing to, but "not able" to work for various reasons, hoping they could remain at the table. But this only made matters worse for them.

Emmanuel addressed this by passing another law stating that anyone who claimed to be unable to work would not only be banned from the table but, would also lose their appetite and ability to eat. This was accomplished by Emmanuel and that Aroma which was everywhere present in his city. Since it was E-man's father who had given everyone the ability to work, if any claimed to be unable it was counted as ungratefulness. And if anyone worked beneath their full potential or against their better judgment, to spite Emmanuel's law, it was counted as unrighteousness.

In these cases, the ever present Aroma would no longer be presented to the ungrateful or unrighteous individual. Without the presence of the Aroma, there would be no appetite and without an appetite, in Emmanuel City, no one ate a single thing because they ceased to be convinced of their need for soul's food. They would then lose their desire for it and with it, the joy of belonging to this new community and fellowship. Thus, the passing of this new law drastically reduced the number of people who tried to avoid honoring Emmanuel through work and service.

However, this law, also, eventually led to some confusion and quite a bit of animosity. It began when a few individuals around the unending table noticed that there were several guests who never got called away from Emmanuel's presence but always remained seated, enjoying Emmanuel's rest and, no doubt, beholding his beauty which was hidden in the light. And Emmanuel himself seemed to take special delight in these individuals. The question was raised as to why these guests were not being called away like the rest.

But soon, word began to spread that these were those who had spent much of their lives serving

Emmanuel's father back in the Nameless City or even back during the days referred to as "The Time Before," when Hue-man and Evelyn's children were trapped living in the Underground Mall—that is, before E-man became Newman and freed them. By their labor, it was said that, these faithful individuals had stored up treasure for themselves in Emmanuel City, and the chief treasure was to behold him. It was now time for others to work and for these few, dedicated servants to rest.

Around the unending table, whenever E-man was silent, his guests traded stories about how they each came to leave the Nameless City and travel up the great hill. Those who lived in The Time Before were asked many questions by the others; questions like, 'What was it like living in that place?' and 'Did anyone ever try to escape and get pass Curse and Consequence?' or 'How did you end up here with us if only those who made it to the top of the hill, or trusted in Newman's name were invited to this table?' But hardly any of the guests from The Time Before had a good answer.

They each remembered trying and trusting their own efforts and failing miserably. Many of them remembered the different attempts they had made at trying to come up with the ingredients to make Emmanuel's meals in the mall. Most admitted failing at this but some claimed to have succeeded. Nonetheless, even when they did, they had no appetite for his cuisine and could not stomach the taste. Had they been able to do so, the Aroma would have changed the air about them and made them unappealing, even nauseating to the lions outside of SOUL FOOLED. But because of their heredity, because they took after Hue-man, they could not acquire the taste for soul's food and were forced to either face those cruel lions alone, or else remain in the mall until help came. Considering this, the guests from The Time Before turned to Emmanuel and asked, "How did you secure a place for us at this table when we had no appetite for soul's food?"

But E-man would not answer them; not yet. He delayed his response for two reasons. First, he thought about those whom he called "the watchers." The watchers had, for a long time, ever since the beginning, been looking with great interest into all that Emmanuel was doing on behalf of those his father chose to rescue from the lions. He knew that they would answer the guests' question with great zeal if he invited them to come and tell the story from their privileged point of view.

But, on top of that, Emmanuel did not immediately answer the question about 'The Time Before' because he knew that there was another controversy developing at his table which he desired to address first. This controversy was not about the blessed ones who were permitted to always remain seated at E-man's table. It was, rather, about the one guest who kept getting up to leave it.

Every time there was a request for volunteers to serve in the rebuilding of Emmanuel City, one individual in particular was always the first to respond. In fact, even before the request for volunteers came, this particular individual's hands were already in the air. It seemed as if he always stayed in a position ready to lift his hands higher. Others around the table began to wonder if, perhaps, the reason he volunteered so much was because there was some extra reward to be gained by doing so much work. Was this individual trying to store up treasure for himself or, maybe, secure a seat at the table from which he would no longer have to rise in order to serve Emmanuel? And, if so, how did he know about this extra reward? Did E-man tell some people about it and not others?

When this particular guest got up from the table for what seemed like the 100th time, he heard others questioning his volunteerism. But he did not want to address their remarks himself. Just then, Emmanuel called to him, "Friend, I'd like to tell your story. I know how you feel about it and that you don't want any attention given to your past. But I was present in your past. So I wouldn't just be telling your story, but my story through yours." The man lifted his hands higher and said humbly, "All stories are about you. I just wish mine didn't take so long to show it. But please, wait until I'm gone and then, tell as much of our story as you'd like."

Emmanuel waited for him to leave and then began telling the man's story, a story very similar to the one which you are about to read. However, there are certain details that E-man did not recount for his hearers, for he rightly saw that they did not need to know such things.

But I, on the other hand, will not be as selective in my telling of this account. For it might be that some of these details will be the very key to help you, the reader, find, or better appreciate, the place reserved for you around the unending table.

Episode 1

SOMETHING I ATE

Twenty years after the deaths of Tru-man and Jermaine, and almost a full twenty years before Emmanuel returned to reclaim and rename the city; back when his other name, Newman, was not allowed in Nameless City, the ambassador from the Chain Linked Nation, Mr. Screwtate, introduced his plan to turn a large number of homes into Halfway's-house fast food restaurants. This plan, as you might recall, involved buying houses from the citizens of Nameless City, with a commitment to secure a place for those residents to live in the condos being built beyond the great hill. This was all a lie, of course, for Screwtate had power neither on the great hill nor beyond it.

Nonetheless, while these fictitious condos were supposedly being built, temporary housing was provided in the form of group-homes for those who took the Screwtate deal. This seemed like a reasonable, short-term solution. However, the short-term kept getting longer and the group-homes soon became overcrowded. Not only that, but they were mostly poorly maintained and thus, quite the hazardous place to live. The plumbing, wiring, fixtures and utilities seemed to have only been halfway prepared for such heavy usage. This led to great and constant conflict between the tenants and those who were in charge of managing the buildings.

But there was one neighborhood where the group-homes saw a significantly lower number of complaints than the rest. This was all because of the brilliant work of one maintenance attendant who was known around the city only as 'the Handy-man.' Like many people in Nameless City, this Handy-man only sought to fix things halfway. But, because of his great skill and ingenuity, even his half-hearted labor was better than most people's full-fledged effort.

It was a humid, sunny summer day (for the city had not yet begun to frost) when the Handy-man showed up to building #152, armed with a large supply of twine, an assortment of screws and a ladder. On this visit, he aimed to rig up a fix for the ventilation system in a row of family-units on the second floor. Unlike the other maintenance attendants in the group-homes, the Handy-man's fixes were not just short-term. They could hold up for quite some time but, only as long as he was there to keep a keen eye on things; to turn and tighten a screw here or there every once in a while.

The duct work in the building was rather shoddy and had begun coming undone in several places. Mr. Screwtate did not own the buildings and so he would not shell out any money for new airways. He left that to the owners and building managers who continued to blame him for not paying enough in rent for the tenants whose homes he had acquired.

But, the Handy-man kept things cool in his buildings. He had fixed up most of the air ducts and would periodically replace the screws or cords as he deemed necessary. Such was the case on this particular day. As he arrived and made his way up the stairs, he took a mental note of all the new problems being reported to him by the tenants he passed in the hall. "No air and no water – unit 1F," an older woman informed him." "I'll get right on it," came his usual response.

He took his time and spent about half the day laboring on the second floor from one unit to the next. Still, he only did about half of the work he could have done. When he decided that he had done enough for one day, he climbed down from his lift and began packing up his work supplies. But, as he folded up his ladder, he noticed a hole in the floor through which he could see right into the unit beneath him. The older woman living there called up to him, "'be nice if you could fix that hole. But more important, we ain't got no air down here. And the water across the hall works today, but mine don't."

"Unit 1F?" he recalled.

"Mmm hmmm," she moaned.

As the Handy-man looked down through the torn floor board, he saw the cutest thing—a little girl, around eight years old, standing directly beneath the hole with her head tilted back and her little mouth open wide.

"And what are you doing?" he asked.

"Please," she said. "Bring a drop of water from the sink and let it drip down. It's so hot down here. Aren't you here to bring us some relief?"

This touched the Handy-man. So much, so that he did not end his workday as planned. Instead, he went down to their unit and worked on the air duct and plumbing late into the evening, until both were restored. When he had finished, he was famished and so were the occupants of unit 1F. He looked at the little girl and her grandmother, Mrs. Coalman, whom everyone simply called 'Mrs. Coal,' and offered to treat them to dinner. Both of them jumped at the offer since, they too felt as if they could eat to the last morsel of an endless buffet. And so, they left the building together, headed for the place where most hungry people in Nameless City went; the only place that could halfway satisfy their ravenous appetite.

It was around 9:30 at night when they finally arrived at Halfway's. The lateness of the hour, however, did nothing to change the fact that they would have to stand outside in the long, serpentine line before they could get in to order their meal. While in line, The Handy-man and Mrs. Coalman found one another's dot in their instant-thought-connectors and each wrote kind words on the other's dot-display-page.

The line was moving slowly and as they waited, the little girl, whose name was Treasure, fell asleep and ended up in the Handy-man's arms when her grandmother could no longer bear her up. Both he and Mrs. Coalman were glad that Treasure was not awake for 'the discussions.' The discussions were new happenings in Nameless City. It seemed that no matter which Halfway's-house a person traveled to, the wait in line now almost always included having to listen to people debate about whether or not the food at Halfway's was healthy and whether or not there was some suitable alternative to it.

Sometimes the debates were comical. At other times, things got quite heated and rather dangerous for those questioning the nutritious nature of what was being served inside. Every once in a while, a manager from the Halfway's-house would come out and kick the 'agitators' out of line. "If you have such a problem with the food," they'd yell, "then starve!"

Soon after this trend began, suspicion began to grow that, perhaps, these agitators were N.I.N.T.E. members who were out to persuade people not to eat at Halfway's. "Pull up your sleeves," the crowds would demand, "and let us see your chains." The debaters would then proceed to show their wrists, both still bound in chains. This would usually put an end to the thought that these individuals might be affiliated with Newman. But that suspicion, despite the lack of evidence to support it, was entirely correct.

Even though Tru-man and Jermaine were now on the other side of the great hill, having died and gone to be with Newman, the N.I.N.T.E. was still very active. The city had built a food-court at the end of Straight Street and stationed agents there to interfere with and discourage citizens from traveling up the hill, and no one could go without an escort. Because of this, many of the current members of the N.I.N.T.E. had not gone up to the top, to Newman's table. As a result, many of them still had both hands chained. But they used this to their advantage in order to blend in and prolong their freedom while they carried out new N.I.N.T.E. initiatives—such as, the discussions.

These discussions were carried out in two different ways by two different groups of N.I.N.T.E. members: those who were called "Door Jams" and those who were called "Insiders." Each thought their way was better and the two groups very rarely worked together on this particular mission. The Door Jams would wait in the line outside of the restaurant but would not actually go in to sit with other customers, for fear that they might be tempted to order and eat the Halfway's cuisine. But the others, the Insiders, would go all the way in but always tried to order the most harmless thing on the menu. They were, however, forced to live with whatever after-effects came along with the meal they chose.

The Handy-man hated hearing the discussions. Not for any reason other than that they disparaged certain meals served at the restaurant which were actually his favorites. Or, rather, meals that he believed *would* be his favorites if he could ever taste them. For he was not yet able to afford all that he truly desired from Halfway's. But some day he would be able to enjoy it all—just not tonight, or any other night, any time soon.

Over the next couple of months, the Handy-man, Mrs. Coalman and the young Treasure became good friends. They would get together often for a meal at the restaurant. But based on the rumors circulating about Halfway's food, they would always order smaller portions whenever they were together. This was a precautionary measure, for they did not want the after-effects of a Halfway's meal to jeopardize their friendship. This was, probably, wise since Mrs. Coalman noticed that she was always more manipulative after having her favorite meal. And the Handyman's usual dish seemed to unleash the vindictive side of his nature.

Most relationships in Nameless City began this way—with people eating less while together at Halfway's, and then, gradually, getting comfortable enough to eat more and more around one another. But the more they allowed themselves to feast freely with their friends, the worse off the relationship grew. Unfortunately, over the course of time, this is just what took place between the Handy-man and the occupants of unit 1F.

It happened this way. One unsuspecting day, the Handy-man arrived at the building to do some routine maintenance. When he saw Treasure running in the hall, he pulled out a gift that he had purchased for her. It was a popular children's toy known as a 'coloring nook'. This was an electronic coloring book where images could be drawn on a number of different screens and then controlled with verbal commands. All of the screens, containing their different images, could then be layered one on top of another to produce a single, composite portrait, even though each item in the portrait was still actually by itself, on its own page. The goal was to see how many pages of images one could create and control all at the same time. The Handy-man knew that Treasure would love it and play with it for hours. And she did.

Later that evening, the trio went to Halfway's together, as usual. After considering how nice it was for her friend, a modest maintenance attendant, to buy such a nice gift for her granddaughter, Mrs. Coalman decided that she would trust the strength of their friendship to be able to withstand the potency of what she normally placed on her plate. They waited in the long line outside the restaurant and, eventually, were ushered inside where they sat down and placed their orders.

When the Handy-man saw that Mrs. Coalman had upgraded her meal, he too decided to order the selection he was used to making when at the diner alone. Then, like usual, the Handy-man got up and left the table for several minutes. The young Treasure awoke to order something from the kid's menu and then, restlessly repositioned herself as she tried to return to her sleep. This was the usual routine. But on this particular night, as the child changed positions and noticed the Handy-man standing over by the dark, red door towards the back of the diner, she did not remain seated like usual. Instead, she slid out from their table and went over to ask, "What's behind that door, Handy?" The Handy-man grabbed her hand and moved back as the door opened and almost hit them square in the face. A couple came out from behind the dark, red door, looking as if, whatever their meal was, it had hurt them to consume it.

"Are those people gonna to be okay?" Treasure asked.

After the couple staggered by, the Handy-man answered, "Yeah, I'm sure they'll be fine. They looked hurt but I think it was a good kind of hurt. You know?"

She shook her head in the negative, "I have no idea what that means."

He laughed and took her back to her grandmother and rejoined them at their booth. As usual, while they waited for their meals to be served, the Handy-man kept turning around to study the red door and the individuals coming and going through it.

"V.I.P.," Mrs. Coalman commented. She added, "Only the fancy chains get to go in there. Think you'll have that kind some day?"

The Handy-man responded, "If I'm lucky. It's all I dream about. But even my dreams would be better if I could just see their menu and know what it is they serve in there. I listen to the songs and what they say about it in the media but I don't know if it's really like that."

"Must be," she opined. "Treasure, why don't you go use the restroom before the food comes out," she said in order to remove her young ears from the conversation. Once Treasure was gone, Mrs. Coal continued, "I had a husband once, years ago. He used to go into the V.I.P. rooms. Boy, did he enjoy it in there! But, when he'd come back out . . . he was really terrible to me for weeks at a time after eating there. I thought he would leave me to go spend all his time dining in V.I.P. but, eventually, I left him. I couldn't take it. And I knew I couldn't take him from it. So that was that. Same thing happened to Treasure's mother, except it was her husband, my son, who decided to leave them for whatever's in there. My only hope is that Treasure breaks this sad cycle."

At first, hearing this made the Handy-man feel ashamed for wanting so desperately to taste the treats which lay behind that door. But then, he thought to himself, "That food in there must be of the most fantastic sort if it's powerful enough to make a man be okay with losing his family!" He did not communicate this, of course, but he now desired to gain entrance all the more.

After halfway enjoying their meal, they left the restaurant and began heading home. While on the way, Mrs. Coalman tried, unsuccessfully, to persuade the Handy-man to do some extra work in her unit while neglecting some of her neighbors. When he refused, she began questioning whether or not he really cared for her and especially, for Treasure, since he was not willing to make their lives better by performing her requests. He rejected her reasoning and in doing so, offended her. She, in turn, insulted him and attempted to humiliate him in front of the little girl.

"You'll never get fancy chains with your attitude, you know? They don't give them to maintenance men. Especially men who don't have anything to offer. You come to Halfway's with an old lady and a little girl every time. They don't want that behind the red door. But with your salary, without us, you'll always be alone. Eating at the tiny tables out front. How does that make you feel?"

The Handy-man responded by shouting obscene things at her and speculating, "I'll never work in your unit again! You're horrible. I bet that's why your husband chose the V.I.P. room over you. You're probably the reason why Treasure's father left her mother too for whatever's behind that dark, red door!"

He said this to injure the woman's heart but did not think about the damage this would cause to the young girl. The little Treasure ran over and kicked the Handy-man in the leg, just north of his knee. She would have kicked him harder and higher but her grandmother pulled her away at the last second. Mrs. Coalman vowed that no matter what future problems she might have in her unit, as long as she lived in the group-homes, she would never call for his help again. The Handy-man walked off mumbling spitefully, "Don't worry, I'll fix you."

The next day, he woke up with a heart full of regret but had to concentrate to remember where the painful emotion had come from. He saw the bruise on his leg and then remembered his argument with the woman from unit 1F. He thought to himself, "Was it something I said?" Then he remembered the meals he and his dinner guests ordered at Halfway's. He put his chained hands over his eyes and shook his head as he concluded, "No, it was something I ate."

An Interlude:
Back Around the Table

Back around the unending table, Emmanuel's guests were hanging onto his every word as he told his tale. But the Star-crowned Storyteller paused for a brief moment as several individuals returned to the table and informed a handful of others that they had been summoned to work in the city. The guests looked at Emmanuel, hoping to receive a pardon that would exempt them from having to leave in the middle of the story. But he assured them that, if they hurried, by the time they returned, they would not have missed the best part. And so, they scurried off to perform their labor of love.

Then, Emmanuel called for more food to come forth from the Living Table and his guests received it with thanks-giving. Now, they waited to see with what sentences he would season the meal. He looked at every one of them and asked, "Shall I continue with the Handy-man's ordeal?" "Please," they implored him. And so, back to the drawing board he went. And that, I mean quite literally; for, as I'm sure you will recall, whenever E-man spoke about the past, the very air in his presence cooperated with his will in order to depict his diction. Those who heard him could literally see what he was saying.

Now, for Emmanuel, one word is worth a thousand pictures. However, my task is to paint just one clear portrait with thousands of words. So, picture if you will, our Handy-man back in the Nameless City, just five short years after we left him last.

Episode 2

What Needs Fixing

By this time, the number of Halfway's-house restaurants in the city had nearly doubled and, more people were being crowded into the group-homes. But the supposed condos beyond the great hill were still nowhere near complete. This being the case, the Handy-man's popularity grew to epic heights as, everywhere he went to work, living in the group-homes became not just bearable, but preferable.

In fact, his service was so noteworthy that, even Mr. Screwtate seemed to be obliged to show the Handy-man an uncharacteristic display of gratitude. To repay him for lessening the complaints coming from the residents of the homes, Screwtate took the Handy-man out to dinner at the food-court at the end of Straight Street. This was a real treat for any citizen of the city, for with Screwtate, there would be no standing in the long lines out front. On top of that, the Handy-man felt that this was about as close as he was going to get to seeing what happens behind the dark, red door.

On the night that they were scheduled to dine together, they arrived separately and met out front. The Handy-man had polished his rusty, old chains, hoping that he would not look too out of place standing beside the Ambassador. After posing for a few press photos with the Chain Linked leader, he followed Screwtate inside to be seated. He was disappointed to see that Screwtate led him to a booth and not to the crimson doorway at the back of the establishment. But he knew that it was in his best interest to, at least, appear grateful; for everyone was aware of how horribly Screwtate took it whenever one of the very few gifts he gave was in any way second guessed. So, the Handy-man followed him to their small table and tried to fake contentment. Ironically, this pretense was the first time he had ever come close to looking more than halfway satisfied at Half-ways.

But Screwtate noticed his soul's dissatisfaction. He had become a master at producing in others the very disappointment the Handy-man was trying to hide. And, while the ambassador enjoyed seeing this disappointment, he too faked a facial expression for his dinner guest; one of genuine concern. He asked, "Tell me, what's the matter? I won't hold anything against you. Just don't lie to me."

The Handy-man's eyes glanced over at the rouge door. He then confessed, "It's just that, I thought all of the important people in the city ate back behind that door. And I thought for sure that, if I was with 'the great Mr. Screwtate', I would get to go back there but . . . Please, forgive me. I don't wanna seem ungrateful."

Then Screwtate warned him, "Listen, because you've been very useful to me very recently, I'm going to overlook your ingratitude. But after tonight, consider yourself fully repaid. It'll be a long time before you ever earn my kindness again." He was about to get up and leave him there but just then, Screwtate thought about the situation and quickly realized that, instead of chastising the Handy-man, he could actually use him to learn something new about the children of Hue-man as it relates to their appetite. Screwtate was always learning.

He changed his tone and asked, "Do you know what it takes to get behind that door?"

The Handy-man responded, "Of course. Everyone knows; no chain, no gain. Gotta have the shiny links to get back there."

Screwtate probed, "But do you know how people get those shiny chains?"

"No. I mean, I hear what they say in the media but, c'mon. That can't be true, right?"

Screwtate thought about encouraging him to go down to Gehenna to throw himself into the fires. But he knew that many people in the city liked and looked up to the Handy-man. So he figured he would get more use out of destroying him in another way. The Handy-man would become a test subject for one of Screwtate's new schemes.

"I can't speak on what the media does," he responded. "But let me ask you. Do you even know what it is that we serve back there?"

"No," the Handy-man said sadly. "But I just know it's gotta be better than what they serve out here. I mean, men have left their whole families for that food.

And you have to have flashy chains just to be invited in! I'd do anything to get back there."

At that point, Screwtate began to test his theory. He leaned across the tiny table and told the titillating secrets of the V.I.P. room. As he spoke, he watched closely to see just how excited the Handy-man became at simply hearing these details. When he saw how entranced he became—the blank look in his eyes, the perverted smile on his face, the Handy-man lowering his hands to rest them on his stomach—he knew that his scheme would have tremendous success.

He ceased from revealing his secrets and sat back in his seat. Looking across the table, he condescendingly told the Handy-man to, "Wipe your mouth. You're drooling." Screwtate tried to hide his disgust, for even though it was only the countless chains beneath his coat which kept him from fully indulging his own every evil impulse, still, Screwtate hypocritically despised Hue-man's children for their foul appetite, their gluttony and lack of self-control. He began to look for a reason to end the evening earlier than planned. Several minutes later his connector began to buzz and, this, he used as his excuse to exit. The Handy-man walked him to the door, hoping, perhaps, that he could get Screwtate to reveal some insight into how people get those shiny chains needed to access the V.I.P. room.

Screwtate wanted him to have those flashy chains, but not yet. He desired that the Handy-man should be much more addicted to the idea, much more ensnared by what happens behind the dark, red door, before he gained entrance. It would be a methodical process to bring him to this point. But everything in the meantime would be used to make the flashy chains being fitted for him that much heavier and harder to wear when he finally got them.

As they reached the door of Halfway's, the Handy-man finally figured out how he would ask Screwtate about getting those chains. But he did not get to make his request because of what was happening just outside the restaurant. There was an agitator in the crowd stirring up trouble in a discussion. Screwtate had thrown agitators out of the line before, but this was the first time that the Handy-man was there to see such a confrontation.

The crowd went silent when they realized that Screwtate was coming out. But the agitator got louder asking, "When have you ever seen Mr. Screwtate do anything in moderation? Yet, for some reason, he won't go into the dark, red room. Hmmm, I wonder why that is? Why is that Mr. Screwtate?"

The Handy-man thought for sure that he was about to witness something very close to murder as Screwtate walked over to the man. As he got close, the crowd parted and moved away from the agitator. Screwtate then lifted his massive hands as high as his chains would allow. He grasped the man's arms firmly and told him in his distinct voice, "Go home Her-man." And then . . . nothing. Surprisingly, Screwtate did nothing except to continue walking away from Halfway's. The Handy-man folded his arms and thought to himself, "So *that's* Her-man. I finally get to put a face to that name." Everyone in Nameless City knew about Her-man, but very few people had actually spent any time with him because of his position or, rather, because of his pedigree.

This gave the Handy-man an idea but, he could not give the idea too much attention because, at that moment, his connector began buzzing with a message that he was truly shocked to see. In Nameless City, almost everyone who lived in a group-home was a fan of the Handy-man—almost everyone. There was one past client who swore to never contact him again, no matter what type of help she needed in her home. But, now, there was something that this client believed only he could help to fix. And so, her communication came: *Hey Handy, long time no see. I know I haven't spoken to you in a while but we've been following your success and I just wanted to congratulate you. Message me back when you're free.*

"Unit 1F," he thought to himself. He wondered why Mrs. Coal was now reaching out to him. Perhaps she was finally able to get over her pride and apologize to him for her behavior that night, so long ago. Or, maybe, something was really wrong. These thoughts swirled around in his head but he decided that he would not message her back until the next morning. He left the food-court and traveled southbound, heading home. It was a cool night so, the Handy-man did not mind walking. He would have driven his work-truck to the meeting but, did not think it would be appropriate to reach for Mr. Screwtate's hand after stepping out of such a humble mode of transportation.

To help pass the time on his way home, he turned on his instant thought device which lit up and connected him to endless entertainment. He tuned in to it but right in the middle of one of his favorite songs, the screen went blank and the device shut off.

What Needs Fixing

When he turned it back on, the screen flashed with the words, *N.I.N.T.E. Digital Book: click here to read.*

The Handy-man quickly exited out of the screen and reloaded his music playlist. He hated when those "alerts" popped up; almost everyone in Nameless City did. Most people tried to ignore these electronic reminders of Newman and his friends whenever they appeared. But thanks to the talented work of Angelique, these reminders continued to present themselves and it would be several more years before the media center found a way to prevent the Preser-V virus from producing new pop-up ads.

Frustrated by this digital disruption, the Handy-man was not paying attention when he stepped into the street. Suddenly, a bright light flashed upon him. At the very last second, he looked up and jumped back onto the sidewalk just before he was hit by a northbound city utility vehicle. Realizing that he could have been killed just then, in his rapidly beating heart, he sent a silent "thank you" toward the top of the hill. Not because he had any idea of whom it was that resided there. But only because, in Nameless City there was a longstanding superstition, a deep-rooted, subconscious awareness that all unexplainable, good things, the *really* good things, did not come from

Gehenna (as the media maintained), but from the highest hilltop.

As he watched the municipal truck continue on its way, he noticed that it was hauling something he hadn't seen for quite some time in Nameless City – lumber. He remembered seeing the trees being cut down and hauled away back when he was a teen. However, he did not remember what the reason was for this herbicide. After a quick search on his connector, he found the answer and concluded, 'either they're moving the trees for better storage or, this coming winter is going to be the extremely cold one they were worried about almost twenty years ago.' But, as long as the city was prepared, he felt he had no reason to worry and, so, he closed the case in his mind.

The next morning, the Handy-man was awakened by the aggressive vibration of his connector. It was another instant thought from the woman in unit 1F: *I'm sorry to bug you. And I understand if you don't want to speak to me. But I have a problem here and I really believe that you're the right man for the job.*

He responded with: *I'm sorry I didn't get back to you last night. I've gotta come by your building today around noon. I'll see you then if you're there.* After his usual morning routine, he loaded up his truck with the day's supplies and then began making his rounds. He thought hard about what could possibly be wrong in unit 1F, for even though Mrs. Coalman had not called him to fix anything in the last five years, his handy-work was nonetheless very present in her unit.

By the time he arrived at building #152, his curiosity was eating him alive. He went to the ground floor apartment and knocked, making his presence known. Mrs. Coalman came to the door while he tried his best to look patient and unconcerned. She smiled and invited him in. As he entered, they each made an effort to hug one other but, their chains got in the way. The Handy-man scanned the apartment, as if he was looking for something specific.

"You're trying to see what needs fixing." she observed. He responded, "Well, you called on me. Last time we spoke you said you wouldn't call on me no matter what kind of help you needed in here. So, the fact that you did ... something's gotta be really wrong. But, I don't see anything around here that needs me?" She informed him, "That's because 'what needs you' isn't here right now. But she'll be here in a minute."

He knew instantly what or, who, Mrs. Coalman was referring to but could not imagine what his fixing abilities had to do with anything. She sat down in her worn spot on the couch and then asked, "You still dreamin' bout that dark, red door?" The Handy-man did not respond. She continued, "Treasure is thirteen years old now. She just got her chains about two months ago. Woke up one Thursday morning and there she was, standing at the foot of my bed wearin'em. The one on her left hand isn't that long. You know what that means don't you? I don't know why I thought, maybe, my grandbaby wouldn't need those rusty chains. But she got'em just like the rest of us. And I'm already startin' to see why."

"Hey, look Mrs. Coal. Like you said, we all get chained. She'll get used to'em. And even if she's having a hard time now, or giving you a hard time now . . . it'll be alright. She's a good kid."

"Is she? Is any one of us really good? My mother thought I was, at first. And I thought that I deserved much more freedom; that I should have had many more links to the chain on my left hand then what I got; that was until I saw how I reacted once I got that Halfway's food in me. And it wasn't even just the food. I'm tellin' you Handy. There's something inside of me that craves that food. The older I get, the more thankful I am for these chains. I don't even want'em gone unless whatever it is inside of me is gonna be gone too."

The Handy-man looked at her in disbelief as he cautioned, "You're startin' to sound like a Free-hand. I've never even talked to one but that sounds like something they'd say." Mrs. Coalman then mumbled something that sounded like, "I wish." She went on, "Anyway, the reason I contacted you is because, I think that you could really be a good influence on Treasure. How old are you Handy?"

"I'm thirty-seven."

"That's perfect. You don't have any children do you? I think Treasure and her friends need something like a father figure. You're successful. You've got a good reputation. You don't even have flashy chains but people respect you."

But he cut her off to correct her, "People don't respect me. They need me. People who're not living in the group-homes don't even know I exist. I'm a glorified janitor. These kids won't listen to me." But she stood up to move closer to him. She looked him in the eyes and said, "You have to. Something you said to Treasure that night, years ago, has grabbed a hold of her. And these young boys out here are just waiting to take advantage of her. I think it's your responsibility to show her something different. You owe it to her."

The Handy-man wanted to ask her what she meant but, just then, the door burst opened and the teen-aged Treasure burst in. She saw the Handy-man and smiled an innocent smile. He, too, smiled and made a generic comment about her girly glamor and teenaged cuteness. This comment meant a lot to her.

"How's your leg?" Treasure asked. He thought for a second and then remembered their last encounter. He had all but forgotten that she was a part of the confrontation that night. "Still healing," he joked. "Dr. said I might need surgery. I'll let you know how that turns out." They all laughed a little harder than what the joke deserved. "We saw you last night, on the family-connector. They showed you on the news having dinner with Mr. Screwtate. How was it?" she asked. He smiled as he remembered the secrets Screwtate revealed, "It was good."

As he looked at the young Treasure, he remembered the little girl who won his heart as she begged for relief through the hole in the ceiling. It now crushed him to think about her getting her little heart broken or her body misused by the grown boys in the Nameless City. At that moment, he spoke to her in his heart, vowing to protect her. Through his smile, she heard his heart and was glad that he had finally come back to visit with them.

"You still got that coloring nook I gave you?"

"Yeah Handy. And it still works too. Wanna see it?"

"Yeah, go get it."

Treasure went to her room to look for the device. While she was gone, the Handy-man told her grandmother, "I'll do it. Don't worry about giving me anything; no spending-money or nuthin'. Just let me know when she's free and I'll make myself available." But Mrs. Coalman wisely responded, "Look Handy, I appreciate you but, if you're gonna do this, you're gonna do it by my rules. I'll give you whatever money you're gonna spend on Treasure. And when she goes with you, she's gotta bring at least one friend. And I'm gonna need you to always have your connector set to 'view me' when y'all are out. I had to take hers away because she wouldn't allow me to view what she was doing when I asked. Listen Handy, you're a nice guy and all. And I wanna trust you. But you've got chains just like the rest of us, and that's not for nuthin'."

He laughed and assured her, "Okay. No problem. But tell me, what did I say five years ago that made such an impression on her?" Mrs. Coalman declined with, "I think that'll be best coming from her. If I tell you, it'll sound trivial. But once you see it in her, you'll know how much it mattered." He settled for her explanation and headed for the door.

Before letting him leave, Mrs. Coalman asked, "Handy, we haven't needed any work done around here for quite some time. Almost five years to be exact. Can you think of any reason why that might be?" The Handy-man smiled a guilty smile and pretended to wonder, "Maybe those old myths are true. Maybe there's somebody up at the top of the hill looking out for you . . . for all of us." He looked up toward the ceiling as if hearing a voice from above. "Newman is that you?" he joked. She laughed and gently pushed him through the doorway and back into the hall as she played along, "Well be sure to thank 'Newman' if you happen to see him out there."

As she closed the door behind him, she thought for a moment. She was sure that the Handy-man was responsible for her good fortune in the apartment.

But then, she wondered, what if there was, somehow, some truth to the joke she had just shared with her old friend. Just what if?

Episode Three
Mr. Nice Guy?
An entire week had gone by and the Handy-man had not yet been back to make good on his vow. But he had every intention of doing so. However, he had become consumed with another task. While he was driving around the city, his connector buzzed with an instant thought. It was from Treasure: *Hey Handy. U forget about me?* He thought to respond with: *Nope. Just been busy. What are you doing right now?* The words appeared on his screen and were instantly sent out to Treasure. Treasure checked with her grandmother and got the "okay" for the Handy-man to come by and take her out. And so, he went by to collect Treasure and her friend.

They hopped up into his work truck without knowing that they had just joined the Handy-man on the mission he had become obsessed with.

"Where are we going?" the frank young lady beside Treasure asked.

"What's your name?" he asked of her. But she would not respond. "What's your friend's name?" he asked Treasure.

Treasure put her arms around her favorite friend (as much as her chains would allow) and announced proudly, "This is my girl Innocence! My grandmom always says, 'you can't get one of us without the other.'"

"Innocence ay?" the Handy-man, repeated. "They call me Handy—short for Handy-man." But Innocence informed him, "Everyone in the group-homes knows who you are."

He decided to have some innocent fun with the girls, and so, he revealed, "And I know who everyone in the group-homes is . . . unit 4C. Right?" The girls looked at each other with amazement and laughed.

"So, if we just give you a name . . . you'll know the unit?" they asked.

"Yup," he confirmed.

For the next ten minutes, the girls gave him names and the Handy-man gave them the unit for each individual; or, in reverse, they gave him a unit number and the Handy-man supplied the names of everyone living inside. When they could no longer name names or conjure up coherent unit numbers, Innocence asked again, "Where are we going?"

There was something special about Innocence. For starters, she said just what was on her mind but never meant any harm. She was curious and caring; naïve in some ways. In fact, she was naïve in the best ways. She knew nothing of malice or mischief. And she always encouraged others to eat the least unhealthy meal on the menu at Halfway's, while she herself hardly ate there at all. But other children were cruel to her. They labeled her a 'weirdo' because she always wore extra-long shirts with big collars or jackets in the summer time. It was as if she was trying to hide some kind of scar or abnormality.

This made Treasure look to separate herself from her girl Innocence whenever they were around their peers. Often, the other girls would gang up on her and dis her for bringing Innocence around them, saying things like, "Nobody needs a 'third-chain' Innocence. Why don't you go somewhere with your 'health-codes'?" "Third-chain" was a term used in Nameless City to identify anyone who sought to put limits on what people ate or did after eating at Half-ways. The "health-codes" were part of an old myth about a recipe for making the perfect meal. No one really believed that such a thing ever existed. However, it did exist and was actually spoken of in the N.I.N.T.E.'s digital book.

Nonetheless, the grown boys in Nameless City liked when the young girls ganged up on Innocence. This was because, every time the girls attacked her, the boys could get Treasure alone. And Treasure was a much different person without her girl Innocence. But, even though the other girls often attempted to injure Innocence, it was always Treasure who ended up getting hurt.

She eventually learned that, if she wanted to protect herself from this harm, she was going to have to fight for her girl Innocence whenever the others tried to separate the two of them. What Treasure did not know, however, was that the other girls only looked to come between them because they too were once friends with Innocence but had abandoned her. And they did not like seeing their old girl Innocence with Treasure.

Now, as the three of them made their way around the city, Innocence was waiting for an answer. The Handy-man knew that he would have to respond to the persistent young lady and, so, he confessed, "For about a week now, I've been driving around looking for a Halfway's-house."

But Treasure wondered out loud, "Halfway's-house? You just passed like four of them while we were playing that name game. What do you mean?"

Innocence added, "If you're looking for one with no line, you might as well forget about it. No matter where you go . . ." The girls finished the sentence together, ". . . there's gonna be a line."

"I know," the Handy-man agreed. "But I'm looking for a certain kind of line." The girls looked at one another, communicating with their eyes that, "something must be wrong with this guy's brain." But then, finally, he spotted what he had been searching for. "There's my Halfway's!" he elated.

"What makes that one so special? What makes *that* one *your* Halfway's?" Treasure asked.

"Because. There's my line."

They looked over and saw an abnormal bulge in the Halfway's normal serpentine line; like a long, large snake in the middle of digesting a gazelle.

"Is that a discussion?" Innocence asked?

"It sure is," he replied.

"Why would you go looking for a Halfway's where the discussions are?"

But he enlightened them, "It's not the discussion; it's who's running it."

After parking the truck, they got out and went to stand in the long line. Fortunately for them, the crowd was so disorganized around the discussion that they were able to slip in at a good place. And even when some in the line protested their intrusion, a couple of city agents who were walking by to keep the peace ordered them to stay where they were. The agitator quieted down while the agents were present. But this was mainly for appearance. He was not actually worried about what they might do to him.

When the agents passed, the Handy-man said to the man who had caused the commotion, "Hey, are you going inside? I know some of you guys don't go inside. But if you're going in . . . when we get in there I'd like to talk to you. I'll even pay for your meal."

"Sorry sir, but I'm not what you think I am. I'm not a . . ." the man looked around to be safe before he said the words, "Door Jam or an Insider, if that's what you're thinking. That's not my scene."

But the Handy-man assured him, "I know who you are, Her-man."

The man replied, "If that's the case then you know I don't need you to pay for my meal. I'll treat you and your young friends."

Her-man dropped his charade and began to cut through the line as if he was royalty. He motioned for the Handy-man to follow him to the entrance of Halfway's. Treasure and Innocence felt like superstars as they enjoyed the preferential treatment.

"So this is what it's like to have flashy chains," Treasure marveled.

They went in right away and got seated. Her-man passed a menu to each of the girls and then looked at the Handy-man and asked, "So what's your deal?" The Handy-man once again looked with great surprise and asked, "You don't eat in the V.I.P. room either?"

"You're the famous Handy-man that had dinner with Screwtate last week aren't you?" Her-man asked.

"Yeah,"

"So let me guess. You didn't get what you wanted from him so now you think you can get it from me? I'm so sick of this."

While they talked, Treasure got up and left the table. Then, Innocence chased after her.

"No, no. It's not like that," the Handy-man tried to convince him. "Your father... I'm sorry. Mr. Screwtate told me some very interesting secrets about the V.I.P. room and I'm just puzzled as to why neither he nor you would want to spend as much time back there as possible. I hear it's fantastic in there."

But Her-man told him, "If there's one thing I've learned, it's to do as Screwtate does, and not as he says."

"What do you mean?"

"If Screwtate wants to get people behind that dark, red door, yet he himself won't go back there. That's reason enough for me to stay out here, eating regular meals like everyone else. And even this food, Screwtate eats sparingly. I think that's how he lives so long and looks so young. So, I only eat a little from Halfway's each time I go. I eat half as much as everyone else and I end up with half as much drama as them too."

"So you don't trust him?" the Handy-man asked.

But, instead of answering him, Her-man asked, "Do you know how I got my name?"

"No."

"Well, my mother once told me that, at first, she wanted to name me after my *true* father. She said that he went up the hill and never came back down. But Screwtate hated my father because of that. So he never wanted to hear my father's name again. Then my mother wanted me to have the Screwtate last name. But you know the law; if the father's last name is known then the child has to have it. Since Screwtate couldn't do anything about that, he *really* hated my father's last name. You know how he hates feeling powerless. So he wanted nothing to do with me, I think, because I reminded him of this one area of impotence in his life. He left me mainly in my mother's care."

"But everyone knows how much he loves your mother. He's always hugging her and smiling whenever she's around. So if he's got all that love for Lady Kakei, he's gotta have love for you too."

Her-man shook his head at the comment, as if to say, 'you couldn't be more wrong.' He then told the Handy-man, "When the city asked him what name they should put on my birth-plate, his response was, 'It's her man, not mine. I don't care what you call it.' He called me an 'it'. He treated me like an 'it' . . . like a thing, my whole life. And that's the way he treats everybody. Newman and his father gave us all two chains. But Screwtate has a bunch of chains under that coat he always wears. And that's not for nuthin'. So, no, I don't trust him."

What Her-man was led to believe about his naming was not too far from the truth. But in actuality, Screwtate gave him that name because he wanted an ever present reminder that no descendent of Hue-man and Evelynne (whom he hated because Emmanuel loved them) was in any real way connected to him. So he demanded that the male child being raised by Kakei be referred to as 'her man.'

"Whoa!" the Handy-man said. "Sounds like you guys have some real family issues. But that's all personal. I'd still like to do some business with him and get behind that red door."

At that, Her-man leaned away from the Handy-man and said, "You know, I thought you were looking for one of *them*. When you approached me in the line, I could've sworn you were trying to get in touch with an agitator or someone from the N.I.N.T.E. initiative. I would have much preferred that over this sickness you have in mind."

"You're working with the N.I.N.T.E.?" the Handy-man exclaimed but then, caught his self as people began to look in their direction. But Her-man could care less.

"No, I'm not. But I appreciate the fact that they don't just swallow whatever is being fed to them. And I see your appetite for what's served in V.I.P. has not just swallowed you but you're also trying to get those young girls over there caught up and consumed by that promiscuous place as well."

"What?" the Handy-man asked. "No I'm not. What are you talking about?"

But Her-man pointed to the back of the restaurant and said, "No? Then why are they back there staring at the dark, red door and trying to get a look at what's inside? You approached me outside because you wanted to know how you could get these girls working in the V.I.P. room. But they're not old enough and you know it! It's eighteen and over. Even

Screwtate doesn't do these kinds of deals in the broad day light. Even he has the sense to be, at least, halfway discrete when he breaks the child-labor laws. Look here, he may enjoy having dinner with you but I can't stomach sitting across the table from you any longer. Buy your own meal and you can go to Gehenna for dessert!"

Her-man got up and stormed away. The Handy-man did not know what he was referring to. He tried to explain himself but could not get the words out fast enough. On top of that, he was just as concerned with Treasure and Innocence over by the dark, red door. Not only was there an age limit to work in the V.I.P. room. There was an age limit to visit there. And for anyone under-age to be allowed to look through the doorway was counted as gross negligence on the part of any irresponsible parent or guardian.

He quickly got up and went to rescue the girls from their curiosity. While they sat back at their undersized table, the Handy-man synced his connector to the screen which waited to take their order. As soon as the two devices were linked, a voice came on announcing, "Congratulations! You've been randomly selected to try one of our brand new recipes featuring artificial flavors from some of our most popular dishes in the V.I.P. room. Choose from or combine any two flavors from the following list."

The Handy-man's heart skipped a beat. This was as close as he'd ever come to tasting what lay behind that dark, red door. But, as he looked at the list of flavors and imagined what delicious delights lay in store for him, Treasure asked, "Oooh, can we have some too?" This was an inconvenient time for him to be selected to sample these savory chef's specialties. He thought about it for a moment. He did not know what after-effects might come from trying these new treats. And with Halfway's, there always seemed to be after-effects.

On top of that, he thought about his conversation with Her-man which confirmed the popular theory about eating smaller portions from Halfway's and experiencing less drama as a result. He decided that, since he was with the girls, he'd better employ this strategy. And, thankfully, it worked. Treasure, however, ate as much as she could while Innocence only picked at her meal. On the way home, Treasure, whose favorite dish always made her a bit rebellious, wanted nothing to do with her girl Innocence who spent the whole time cautioning Treasure against eating so much. She did not speak to Innocence nor even look at her for the entire ride. The Handy-man had some small reactions to the food, but he was able to curtail them, at least until he dropped the girls off.

When he transferred Treasure back to Mrs. Coal, she thanked him and then asked, "Did you forget that I was viewing you the whole time?" The Handy-man had indeed forgotten about this. She continued, "What was that all about with that guy Her-man?"

But he belittled it, "It was nothing. Just a misunderstanding. He thought I was trying to get Treasure and her girl Innocence to work in the V.I.P.; to break the child-labor laws. But I was asking him about my own entrance, not theirs. I would never do that."

Mrs. Coal then asked, "Did Treasure stare at the red door?"

"Yes."

"Just like you used to when she was younger," she reminded him. "She used to watch you stare at it, now you're watching her stare at it."

"Wait, are you saying that I'm responsible for her curiosity? C'mon! All the things that kids get into these days and you're blaming me? You should've seen'em on the way home. Her and that girl

Innocence won't be friends much longer the way she treats her after she eats at Halfway's."

He felt the after-effects from his meal beginning to kick in. This would encourage him to say the hurtful things he was already thinking deep inside. His favorite meal always seemed to make him the more vindictive. But you must not misunderstand. It was not the meal that made him so; for the food only encouraged him to show to others what he himself already was.

"It's not just what you did back then that influenced her Handy, it's what you said; what she heard you say."

"You keep saying that Mrs. Coal but I don't remember what I said. I've gotta go before I do or 'say' something else I'll regret. I'll see you next week."

He took off down the hallway and back out to his truck then began heading home. He was all alone but felt he needed someone upon whom he could release his vindictive aggression. Just then, his connector buzzed with an instant thought from Mr. Screwtate. The Handy-man got excited and pulled over to read the message: *I'd like to go 'head to head,' can you talk?*

The Handy-man thought and sent back: *Of course. You initiate, I'll accept.*

The device buzzed again and lit up. It was the initiation from Screwtate to begin a live, face to face or, screen to screen, conversation. The Handy-man accepted and their chat began.

"I was checking the daily report for Halfway's and I see that you were randomly selected to taste our new recipe with some of the flavors normally reserved for the V.I.P. room. How did you enjoy it?"

This shocked the Handy-man even more. "You make these connections personally?" he marveled. "I thought some low level employee would be doing this kind of work."

"No, this is a new marketing plan and I'm involved in every level of all new plans. So, how did you enjoy it?"

"Uh, actually sir. I didn't. I mean, it's not that I didn't enjoy it. I didn't even taste it because I was with some young people and ... well ... the thing is ... Uhm ... let's see ... how do I say ...."

"What is it? Just say it. I've probably heard it already from someone else so I won't get angry with you," Screwtate tried to reassure him.

"It's just that . . . well . . . you know, they say you shouldn't try new dishes at Halfway's if you have something important to do right after. You kinda need to know how your body is going to react to the food first. And I had these young people with me."

Screwtate fought hard not to let his rage seep through his teeth. He hated hearing criticisms about the Halfway's-house, even though the criticisms were almost always true and only ever, once-in-a-while, over exaggerated. But then the Handy-man added a detail which temporarily distracted Screwtate from his anger.

"Plus I remembered what your son said. I saw him there today."

"My son?" Screwtate questioned implausibly.

"I mean Her-man. I'm sorry."

"That's alright. What did Her-man say?"

"Well, he confirmed what people say about the food; that the way to have less drama is to eat smaller portions. So, that's what I did today."

Screwtate was terribly annoyed when people who usually lacked self-control got a sudden boost of morality and, as a result, failed to fall victim to some trap he had set for them. He almost lost his cool. But

Screwtate was the kind of individual who rarely flew off the handle. Instead, his wicked imagination quickly devised ways to destroy people who made him angry or feel any emotion he did not wish to feel. It was a good thing, for Screwtate at least, that he already had a plan to destroy the Handy-man. But now his plan would expand a bit wider to do just a little more damage.

He was already aware that the Handy-man did not take the taste-test earlier. Not only did his records from the Halfway's-house show this, but Screwtate was also tuned in and watching him through the Handy-man's connector which was set to 'view me.' Screwtate could have picked up his signal easily, since, the Handy-man was broadcasting from a Halfway's-house. Or, because of his relationship with Mr. Conman and the media center, Screwtate could be patched into the right channel and pick up the feed from anywhere and the Handy-man would never know he was being watched. As he monitored him that day, Screwtate liked what he saw in the young Treasure and her girl Innocence. He now included them in his plans to destroy the Handy-man, even though he already had a separate plan in the works to destroy Treasure.

Mr. Nice Guy?

"You know, Handy . . . can I call you Handy? Of course I can. I like you. I want to see you get your shiny chains. I think you'd love it in the V.I.P. room. In fact, you'll never want to come back out if I got you in there. And I'm this close to getting you in. You saw some of the flavors we have back there, didn't you?"

"I did sir. I always thought it'd be something like that but now that I know, you have no idea how bad I want to go in there."

"Well listen to this Handy. In the V.I.P. room, you don't just choose from two flavors. You get to combine as many flavors as you want into one dish. Just imagine that."

As Screwtate talked, the Handy-man began imagining it all. He lost strength in his arms as the blood rushed to the muscles in his stomach, as if he was preparing to digest a meal. Screwtate yelled, "Hey! Hey! Hey! Put your connector back up. Hold it up so that I can see your eyes. I mean . . . I wanna see your face while we're talking."

This was important to Screwtate for, it was by the eyes that he was able to judge the level of hunger—discontentment and desire—in a person's soul. But he had missed this opportunity. He could not see the

Handy-man's eyes and so he did not know how desperate he was at that particular moment. So Screwtate decided to take a chance with his proposition.

"You know Handy, I could get you in but, you've gotta have something to offer. Everyone who gets those chains gives up something, or someone they're attached to. I could send you halfway up the hill and you'd come back with new chains but, you'd have to take something up there, something that means a lot to you, and come back without it. But I don't think you have the stomach for it. You're too much of a nice guy. You couldn't handle this so, never mind."

The Handy-man knew he was being baited. But what was on the hook was too good to pass up just for the sake of pride.

"Nah. I'm not that nice of a guy. I promise."

"Yeah, I hear you talkin'. But, when I see you; I mean, everyone loves you. You work extra hard in the group-homes to help all those people. You spend time with kids in the neighborhood. I hear you're even mentoring some young girls. You're too much of a good guy. I mean, there's a reason the V.I.P. room is eighteen and over. Maybe it's not for you."

Mr. Nice Guy?

But the Handy-man saw his opportunity to kill two birds with one stone. Still looking for a way to express his vindictiveness, he could do that and, at the same time, convince Mr. Screwtate of just how nice he was not, if he confessed some of his deeds.

"You think I'm a nice guy? Well, you know those girls I mentor right? Five years ago I had an argument with the grandmother of one of them. She came out of Halfway's and asked me to neglect the other tenants in her building and work exclusively on her place. I refused and we had words, awful words for each other."

"That's it Handy? You had words with an old woman five years ago? You've gotta do better than that to convince me."

"No, that's not it. Please, listen, sir. She told me that she would never ask me to do another thing in her unit as long as she lived in the group homes. So you know what I did?"

"What'd you do?"

"I fixed her. I fix anyone who crosses me. I did the exact opposite of what she wanted. She's needed me every single day for the past five years more than she could ever know. I rigged it so that all of the solar panels for her building would store up all of the energy the building needs and direct it right into her unit. That much energy, if it's released in the wrong way, would cause such a blast that it would be seen from the top of the great hill. But I rigged it so that every time someone in another unit does anything at all that uses energy – turning on a light, opening a refrigerator door – little by little the energy gets released safely. But if I ever stop working and doing upkeep on the other units around hers, and all that energy gets stored up and released at once, she's 'good for Gehenna.' I also made a bunch of other 'fixes' so that things in her unit only get fixed when I fix the units adjacent to hers. I haven't been back in her apartment for five years but, technically, my handy-work has been on that unit every single day."

Even Screwtate was shocked and impressed by how sinister his scheme was. Upon hearing this, he figured the Handy-man might be ready to make the sacrificial offering he would demand of him.

"Okay Handy. I'm sold. You might be ready for this after all. I'll tell you what I need from you if you're going to get behind the dark, red door. Those girls you had with you today . . . what are their names?"

"One is named Treasure. She's the granddaughter of the woman I was just telling you about." The Handy-man laughed as he thought about the irony of now helping this same woman to raise a child. "The other one is Treasure's girl Innocence. What about'em?"

"Innocence ay? Well, like I said, everyone's gotta give up an attachment to something . . . or someone. When you come into the V.I.P. room, either you leave someone outside whom you will most certainly never see the same way again or, you bring someone in with you. And I decide what happens to that person afterwards. And I think I can use one of those girls in there."

But, having not been able to see the Handy-man's eyes earlier, Screwtate was about to realize that he had miscalculated the situation. The Handy-man had made a vow in his heart to protect the young Treasure, and it was because of this vow that Screwtate almost lost him when the Handy-man reacted.

"What!?! So this is what Her-man was talking about? You really do break the child-labor laws. You think I'm going to give up Treasure for you to let her work back there just so I can get in? You're talking to the wrong man!"

Screwtate looked into his eyes and saw the power of the vow motivating his words, so his wonderfully wicked mind quickly shifted gears. "No. That's not what I'm saying at all. At least, not the way you're taking it. Let me be honest with you."

Now this should have been a dead giveaway that something was amiss. Screwtate was never honest with anyone except for when it benefited his scheme more than it benefited the other person. He fixed his mouth to tell the truth which, for him, was akin to someone preparing to speak a foreign language that they have only just began to learn.

"I saw you in Halfway's earlier today. I was not there but, you're connector must have been set to 'view me.' I was monitoring what was going on in the restaurant and I guess I picked up your broadcast. I saw Her-man accusing you of attempting to bring those young girls in for a job in the V.I.P. room. You wanted to convince Her-man that he was mistaken about your intentions, right? Well, now I'm trying to convince you of the same thing. Don't do me like he did you. Hear me out. Okay?"

Mr. Nice Guy? 73

The Handy-man was thankful that Screwtate had allowed him to have an emotional outburst without being penalized for his disrespect. He also felt that he had won Screwtate's respect in that moment, this gave him a false sense of power in the situation, which Screwtate used to his own advantage. The Ambassador continued, "Listen, I do want those girls to work in the V.I.P. room but, not now. No! Some of my colleagues break the child-labor laws but that's not my scene. I want to wait until the girls are older, over eighteen like the law says. In fact, I need you to do exactly what you already planned to do. Help keep Treasure and her girl Innocence safe for the next couple of years. And then, when they turn eighteen, they'll have a job at Halfway's waiting for them."

The Handy-man, having been lured by the lie, calmed down a bit then said, "That sounds a little better. But I don't know. Why does it feel like I'd still be selling her out if I did what you're asking?"

"Listen. I can see it in your eyes. You've got some kind of attachment to Treasure. So how about we make the deal, not for her, per se, but for her girl Innocence. Surely I can take one without the other. You just have to keep Innocence around until Treasure turns eighteen, and then . . . bring her to the

Halfway's to fill out an application. I'll do the rest of the convincing so it won't be on you."

Screwtate knew that if he had any real chance of getting Treasure or her girl Innocence, he needed to begin setting up traps to ensnare their souls long before they turned eighteen. And while he was also working on this, he had full confidence that his plans for the Handy-man would be enough to engulf them all. And, unfortunately, he was almost entirely correct.

Episode Four
Electrik-Blue

Seasons changed and years passed. The Handy-man continued to be present in Treasure's teenaged life, doing what he could to keep her girl Innocence in the picture. He paid special attention whenever he went by to visit with them. If he noticed Treasure hanging out with other girls, talking reckless about boys or being too concerned about what someone said or did on their connector's dot-display-page, he would encourage her to be different and not so concerned with the trends of the day.

But when Treasure turned sixteen, she stopped hanging out with Innocence for a time and even contemplated ditching her altogether. Concerned for her granddaughter, Mrs. Coalman once again connected with the Handy-man and asked him to come and talk to her from a male's perspective. The Handy-man aimed to encourage Treasure by telling her, "Listen, your girl, Innocence is special. Friends like her don't come along every day. I know you're tired of her always being around cuz she won't let you do what these other girls do. These other girls used to be friends with Innocence too didn't they? But they were quick to abandon her. But I'm tellin' you Treasure, there's gonna come a day when they'll want her back in their lives. They're gonna wish they never let go of her. But just think—you will have had her with you all along and won't have to go trying to get her back. Isn't that better?" And she agreed.

The Handy-man justified this in his mind. He figured that, since he really did believe that what he was saying would help Treasure, he was still keeping the vow he had made to her in his heart; even while he was also keeping his end of the deal he made with Mr. Screwtate. He told himself, 'When Treasure turns eighteen, if she or Innocence or both of them decide to work in the V.I.P. room at Halfway's, then hey, that would be a grown-up decision that I couldn't stop even if I wanted to.' But, little did he know how their decision would be heavily influenced by what he was about to become addicted to. To create this craving in the Handyman, Screwtate had been very busy putting several schemes into effect.

The N.I.N.T.E. had been very successful with the "discussion" initiative. So much so that Screwtate knew it would only be a matter of time before people began seriously questioning the Halfway's meals and, then, start looking for an alternative source of sustenance. Those who led the discussions, very carefully and very cleverly, encouraged people to seek an Aroma beyond the food-court. They did not mention climbing the North hill or the name of Newman and so, with both of their hands still chained like everyone else's, there was no way to prosecute them for treason.

Screwtate knew that there would be an uprising if city agents began arresting people whom they could not prove to be N.I.N.T.E. members. This should have infuriated him since there was really nothing he could do about it and, everyone knew how much he hated feeling or looking powerless.

But Screwtate was not bothered by this in the least. He was a very calculating individual and had planned for this eventuality. Screwtate had not burned all of the trees that the city cut down years ago. He stored them; rather, hid them in a secret location and from time to time, would have the lumber transported to about halfway up the hill; just before the SOUL FOOLED restaurant. He did this in order to supply city workers who thought they were going up to build condos behind the great hill and restore the underground mall but, who instead were really being sent to build a bridge—a bridge that extended to the east hills.

Circulating in Nameless City were strange myths and many mysteries about what happens in the hills. These stories went back as far as anyone could remember. The north hills were, of course, all about Newman; but the east hills had birthed, literally, millions of strange ideas and ideologies. Back during The Time Before, when Newman came to free the children of Hue-man and Evelyn from SOUL FOOLED, most of their children ran down into the city. But some of them had been purposely misguided by the owner of SOUL FOOLED to head toward the east and to make their homes there in the hills. The owner also put into their minds the seeds of all the bizarre ideas that would soon begin to sprout and grow and spread from that direction.

Now, in the course of time, Screwtate saw the need to give the people of Nameless City access to these ideas from the east. And so, he began to build this bridge and had completed it just in time to lessen the impact of the N.I.N.T.E.'s discussions. Anyone who dared to venture up the great hill could be easily detoured to seek soul's satisfaction from the east. Some of the men who worked on the bridge did question the project but they were relieved of their duty and summarily sent to SOUL FOOLED to think it over. But those never returned to work.

This is how Screwtate answered the success of the discussions. But for those who were not deterred by the agitators in the line and who continued to dine at Halfway's, Screwtate had another scheme in the works geared to spice up the restaurant's boring meals. And this is the trap the Handy-man fell into. It happened in this way.

During one of their regular trips to Halfway's, Treasure and her grandmother ran into the Handy-man. But it was the grandmother who first encountered him, for the teen was not near her at the time. "Where's Treasure?" he asked. Mrs. Coalman turned halfway around and motioned with her head as she calmly complained, "Where do you think?" He looked and saw Treasure sitting a couple booths away from the dark, red door, trying to look inconspicuous. Her grandmother called her over and then, they invited him to sit with them.

Once they made it to their table, he asked, "Hey, how's Innocence?"

"She's fine. We were hanging out earlier."

They sat, quite happily, looking over the menu hoping to find something new. And unfortunately, there was a brand new selection at the top of the "adult" section. *Ask about our new Electrik-Blue Room special*, the advertisement read.

This sounded intriguing. When the voice prompt came on to take their order at the table, the Handy-man inquired about the special. He was thrilled when he was told, "Well sir, the Blue Room has been designed for the curiously hungry. We know that many of our guests may never get the flashy chains needed to access what's behind the dark, red door. But we're giving all adult guests an opportunity to see what goes on back there. So, if you're over eighteen, just beneath your feet in our basement, there is a room set up for your viewing pleasure. On a huge screen, you can watch people with expensive chains eat extravagant meals. We guarantee that you will enjoy seeing it just as much as they enjoy eating it." As you may recall, every meal at Halfway's came with some type of guarantee, though none of them ever accomplished their claim.

The Handy-man's face lit up like Gehenna on the weekend. (The trash heap always seemed to burn brighter whenever new garbage was introduced to it.) He tried to sit still and pretend that he wanted to remain at their suddenly uninteresting table. But it was oozing out of him.

"Go ahead downstairs. You're dying of curiosity and it's killing me to watch," Mrs. Coalman said.

He defended himself, "Hey, listen. This is as close to the V.I.P. as I'm probably ever gonna get. Enjoy your meal guys. I'll see you later okay?"

Treasure watched him go, sadly. Off he went to experience his dream – the poor man's V.I.P. As he walked down the stairs, Screwtate watched from his own private viewing area. With each step, Screwtate grew more expectant and excited, like a hungry hunter watching his pray step deeper and harder into a series of snares. The Handy-man descended to the lowest level and it was instantly obvious – he was hooked from that moment on. Even when the Handy-man came back up from that electric, blue basement, his soul was still down there and would be for some time to come.

This became his favorite pastime. In fact, in order to spend more time in that place, he began to work less than half-days but chose to charge more money so as to not miss out on the pay. It soon became painfully clear that his obsession was beginning to affect him in a number of ways. For instance, even though he was doing more watching and less eating in the Electrik-Blue Room, somehow he felt heavier—more weighed down—than before. His time with Treasure was also not the same. He stopped encouraging her to spend time with Innocence. In fact, now, he even saw her differently. He would often picture her wearing one of those cute, little Halfway's uniforms which only halfway concealed what needed to be covered. He used to aim to protect Treasure from others but now, he felt he must protect her from himself.

His addiction had become dangerous in more ways than just that. One night, in the middle of that night, the Handy-man had to be called to the group-home in order to fix one of his 'fixes.' He had spent so much time in the Electrik-Blue Room that he stopped making the adjustments needed to regulate the level of solar power being released by the vindictive vices he had set up in building #152. He got there just in time to save the building and the precious Treasure within it.

Seeing all of the potential harm he could cause, the Handy-man purposely became distant. He felt that he had done enough for Treasure at this point in her life. And besides, his deal with Screwtate might be unnecessary now. 'Who needs the dark, red room?' he thought. The Blue Room might satisfy him just fine.

But, as he began to back away, his lackadaisical mentoring led to an interesting instant thought message from Treasure's grandmother: *Hey Handy. Haven't seen you in a while. Just thought you should know that our little Treasure has not been so selective in her choice of friends lately. And she's got a boyfriend now who has convinced her to totally get rid of her girl Innocence. I'm just hoping you can talk to her.*

"Why me?" he thought to himself. "This will be the last time. I'm not cut out for this." These words showed up on his connector, but he did not instantly send them to Treasure's grandmother. He erased the message and then agreed to take the teen out on the following day. And when the next day came, he did just that.

He went by to pick her up. Treasure hopped up into the truck and the Handy-man asked, "Where's your friend?"

"I haven't seen Innocence in a couple of weeks," she replied.

"I'm not talking about Innocence. I'm talking about your little boyfriend I been hearing about."

She blushed. "Who told you? Never mind, I know who told you. Her and her big mouth."

"Watch it!" he warned. "You're talking about my friend, you know."

"She was my grandmother before she was your friend," Treasure shot back.

They smiled as he pulled around the corner. He took her to the nearest Halfway's he could find so as to keep their outing as short as possible. As they stood in the line, he tried to talk to her about her new boyfriend, about Innocence and all. But he could not find the words.

He asked, "How old are you now Treasure?"

"I'm sixteen. But I'm more than sixteen and a half cuz I'll be seventeen in four months. I want a job. Boys can become junior city agents but what can we do?"

"You can be a junior city agent if you want," he encouraged her.

But she knew that many more males than females were accepted into that program. She asked, "Can you think of any other jobs for someone my age? I mean, soon, I'm gonna wanna buy a car."

In his mind, he chastised himself for thinking of suggesting that she consider working in V.I.P. While he thought this, the chain on his left hand got a little heavier but he was not yet sensitive to the weight, at least, not enough to notice the change. As he stood there, he struggled to find the words to advise her. However, just a few heads in front of them, in the line was a man who would do much more to encourage her. He was part of the N.I.N.T.E. and was preparing to spark a discussion for the hungry crowd. The man's name was Stroughman but the crowds had recently dubbed him Straw-man. This is because he was masterfully skilled at constructing and then demolishing 'straw-man arguments' to silence those who opposed him. This gifted orator was a Door Jam. He had timed the beginning of his speech perfectly, giving himself just enough time to finish before he reached the entrance of Halfway's. But, upon overhearing the Handy-man struggle to help the young girl, Straw-man decided to change the direction of his planned speech.

As he turned to ready himself, someone in the crowd shouted, "Ay it's Straw-man!" Another yelled out, "I knew he couldn't keep quiet. You goin' in this time Straw-man? Or are you just 'goin' in' on Halfway's?" They all laughed. Straw-man laughed along with them and then he began.

"Have you ever noticed that, when it comes to dealing with women, men are like miners? Seriously, they are. Think about coal miners or gold miners. They spend all their time looking for treasures buried deep beneath the surface in the underground mall. And when they believe they've found a place where there's treasure, they will stop at nothing, spare no expense, use whatever tools necessary to get at that treasure and bring it up.

"Men go mining for women all the time. The only problem is, a lot of women don't know what treasures they have to offer. And, if they do, they don't know how to properly bury it. Most of what they have to offer is sitting right near the surface. See, some women think they only have one thing that men are looking for—the treasure of their body. They don't consider the fact that a woman's point of view is a treasure that men need, their time and attention, their commitment and companionship, their strength and support. These are all treasures.

"For most women, all of these treasures are sitting right near the surface and a man doesn't need to pull out many tools at all to get them. He may pull out the tool of compliments or attention. Or he might dig deeper with gifts. Yeah, giving gifts is a digging-tool. He may even use the tool of spending time with her. But he rarely has to dig deep with the tool of honesty, the tool of protection—protecting her from her own emotions and his less-than-honorable intentions, and all men have them. And if he does not have to use any of these tools then you *know* he's not going to pull out the tool of real commitment. Too often, a guy pulls out the tool of compliments or the tool of attention on a woman and all of her treasure just comes spilling out. Listen . . ."

He got close to the door and thought that he would have to wrap up his speech. But even the employee there, who would have normally thrown him out of line by this point, was listening; for he saw the wisdom in Straw-man's argument. The "agitator" wrapped up his mini-sermon. He turned and looked directly at the teenaged Treasure and said to the crowd, "Young ladies, bury your treasure. The deeper you bury it, the more tools he's gonna have to use to find it. And he'll always remember what tool it took to possess what he's found."

This made all the sense in the world to Treasure, for she had already begun to unearth her precious self to her new boyfriend. Straw-man left the line and left those in the crowd to ponder his words. Many of them wanted to applaud but, they did not. They knew that if they showed their support for an agitator, this could be used against them in some future prosecution. But they were each thankful for the 'food for thought' he served them that day. None was more thankful than the Handy-man. This was the first time that he actually wanted to listen to the discussions. In fact, when Straw-man passed him, he seemed to leave a most pleasant aroma in the air. Some people even left the line to follow him or, rather, his scent.

The Handy-man also thought of following in his fragrant footsteps but, he felt it would be irresponsible of him to take the young Treasure away to wherever this Straw-man was going. Besides, what if he was actually part of the N.I.N.T.E.? He figured it would be in their best interest to remain at the Halfway's. How wrong he was.

The line was shorter and the wait, not long at all since several souls left to follow the discussion leader. As Treasure and the Handy-man entered the restaurant, they looked for an empty table. But Treasure saw her girl Innocence over in the corner. She wanted to go say hello and maybe sit and talk with her. To the Handy-man she said, "There's Innocence. Do you mind if I go sit with her?"

"No. I don't mind. I'm going downstairs for a quick minute."

Treasure went to say 'hi' and, perhaps, to invite Innocence to come sit with them. However, when she got close she saw that Innocence was not alone but was there with another group of young girls – girls younger than Treasure. It was an awkward moment but, not for Innocence, for she did not think herself disloyal. It was Treasure who felt some type of way. She knew that she had dissed her girl Innocence several times over the past month.

Treasure looked at the group of girls and waved a very stiff "hello." She was not mad at Innocence. If anything, she was mad at herself. But she was happy that the other young girls would get to benefit from knowing her friend. She told them, "You guys don't know how lucky you are to have Innocence. Don't do what most other girls have done. Don't let her slip away. She's a great friend."

Innocence's eyes began to well up with tears. She felt that this was an unnecessary 'goodbye'. "You can join us Treasure," she said. But Treasure was already backing away. "No. I can't. I'm here with the Handy-man. I've gotta get back to him. I'll see you around, okay?" She turned and went to find her missing mentor.

Without her girl Innocence, Treasure thought to herself that she might be able to appear old enough to be allowed to go downstairs into the Blue Room to get the Handy-man and, maybe, take a peek to see some of the V.I.P. action on the screen. But, to her surprise, the Halfway's employee who was guarding the steep stairwell had stepped away from his post. And so, she quickly slipped through the turnstile then tip-toed down the steps and into the electric, blue haze.

She made it to the bottom of the steps and was about to turn the corner to enter the viewing area but, she stopped first to put her head down and listen to the seductive sounds of the V.I.P. room. She heard the rude way the customers ordered their meals; the crass conversations between the guests as they waited; their costly chains rattling as they ravenously ransacked their food the second it arrived; their teeth ripping apart and chewing everything that was willing (or unwilling) to die for their pleasure; the gulp of every swallow; the slurp of every straw; and also, for some reason, the sounds of people being hurt. She was about to turn that corner and enter the viewing room but just then, her girl Innocence grabbed her arm.

"You can't go in there Treasure. That's not for you."

"Shhhh. Let me go Innocence! I can't spend my whole life doing what you want me to do."

"Treasure do you know how many friends I have? Better yet, do you know how many friends I have lost? If you go around this corner, you'll be one of them cuz

I can't go in there with you. And I know you're not gonna wanna spend time with me anymore after you come out. The Handy-man doesn't even spend time with us anymore since he went down there. I saw y'all come in together but where is he now? In there, right?"

Treasure knew Innocence was right. She did not have to even answer the question.

"Exactly," Innocence concluded. "Look Treasure. I've learned something about myself. It might be hard to have me as a friend. But it's not hard at all to lose me. And then, it's gonna be even harder to win me back. That's only because I don't want to be taken for granted. But I also know this: I'm tired of losing all my friends. Don't be another one."

Treasure snatched her arm away from her childhood friend and turned halfway around. Innocence immediately stormed up the stairs and went back to the table with her young companions. Treasure was now free to do as she pleased. She turned the corner and entered the Electrik-Blue Room and saw some of the most bizarre things she had ever seen. There was a large screen up on the wall in the front of the room. What was on the screen was bizarre in and of itself. From the small glimpse

Treasure took, she could see why men and women were hurting when they came out of the dark, red room. But just as bizarre as what was on the screen, if not more so, is what was happening in the Blue Room itself.

Now, there is nothing quite as silly as this in our world, I'm sure; so you must try to imagine. There were about thirty to forty reclining chairs in the Blue Room. And in those chairs sat mostly men, but also a few women, leaning all the way back. Those who reclined in these chairs seemed to be delusional. Each of them had unbuttoned the top button on their pants, as if, preparing for their stomachs to expand after laboring to consume a large meal. And as they lay back, they lifted their shirts to place their hands on their mid-sections to rub their bellies, as if their stomachs were full of food. But, they were not. How could they be? For there was no food being served in the Blue Room. There was no fulfillment to be had, for they were not the ones eating. They only watched the people with gorgeous chains gorge themselves on the screen. And yet, as they sat there in their meal-less state, they each expressed many "oohs," "ahhhs" and "mmmms" as if they were being delighted by the dishes served behind the dark, red door.

This insanity frightened Treasure. She was looking for the Handy-man in the Blue Room but, also, she thought she might see someone else being featured on the screen in the red room. Perhaps she would check again but she could not bring herself to look back up at the screen. At that moment, the employee from Halfway's at the top of the stairwell shouted, "Hey, are you supposed to be down there?" Everyone, including the Handy-man, turned and looked at Treasure. They were all embarrassed for they imagined how helplessly desperate and happily deceived they must've looked to her. But Treasure, too, was embarrassed for being where she had no business being and seeing what she saw. She darted up the stairs and ran out of Halfway's, back to her grandmother.

The Handy-man fixed his clothes and left the restaurant without even being halfway satisfied. How could he have been? For he did not visit the Blue Room to eat but to be fed a lie. He wanted to go by and explain to Treasure and her grandmother but could not think of how he would do so. On top of that, he was already looking for a way to exit Treasure's life. Perhaps this pain would be sharp enough to cut their tie.

He drove around the city, thinking it all through. He thought that, if only he had his shiny chains, all of his problems would be solved. He would not be in the Electrik-Blue Room. Instead, he would be comfortably lounging in the V.I.P. and there would be no shame in that. He could combine all those dangerously delicious flavors and finally be fulfilled. While he comforted himself with this fantasy, he got an instant thought from Screwtate: *I'd like to talk to you tonight. I'm wrapping up some business at one the group-homes. Can you meet me in front of the buildings on Broadway?*

The Handy-man confirmed and then realized that the group-homes on Broadway were the ones which housed Treasure and her grandmother. He rushed over to the location and saw Screwtate coming out just as he was pulling up. He quickly parked his truck and then anxiously made his way over to meet the ambassador from the Chain Linked Nation.

"Hey. How you doin' Mr. Screwtate? Everything alright? What brings you down here?"

"Well, if you must know, I had some complaints about people fighting over space in here. So I wanted to see about it. I'm thinking of buying this building and turning it into a Halfway's once the condos are ready. And remind me Handy, since when do I owe you an answer for anything that I do?"

"No. You don't owe me an answer at all. I'm trippin'. I'm sorry. But you wanted to meet with me right?"

"Yeah Handy. But you'd better remember your place." Screwtate took a second and let his anger subside and then continued, "Anyway, I was thinking, 'you know what? Why wait until the girl turns eighteen to keep my end of the deal.' You've been diligent on your end, keeping Treasure's girl Innocence in the picture and all but, that's really a lot to ask of you. I mean, you're not the girl's father right? So, here's what you're gonna do. Get your stuff together. Get all your affairs in order. Get someone to maintain these buildings while you're gone and head up to the food-court at the end of Straight Street. Tell the city agents stationed there that I sent you up the hill. They'll give you very specific directions which you must follow if you want those expensive chains. You will go halfway up the hill. And there you will meet with my boss and talk about your new chains. When you get back, if you get back, you come and see me."

Screwtate's timing was perfect. The Handy-man was now properly addicted to the idea of getting behind the dark, red door. He felt bad enough about his self that this opportunity to change his chains seemed like it could have been a gift from the hilltop (that is, if the one who lived up there was actually responsible for giving good gifts, and also, if this turn of events could actually be called a 'good gift' in the first place). Screwtate saw the desperation in his eyes and knew that the Handy-man would make the trip halfway up the hill. He patted him on the shoulder and walked away followed by the ornamental city agents who always decorated his presence.

The Handy-man went inside to tell his good news to Treasure and her grandmother. He wanted them to know that he would not mistreat them or abandon them like the other men in their lives once he got his new chains and gained access to the V.I.P. room. He knocked on the door, expecting first that he would have to explain himself for the embarrassing episode at Halfway's earlier. But Treasure opened up the door and excitedly screamed, "I got a job!"

"What?" He said, sounding slightly confused. Treasure and her grandmother both smiled enthusiastically. Treasure explained, "Mr. Screwtate was just here, just before you came. He gave me a job!"

The Handy-man thought of what this must mean. Did he fail in his vow to protect Treasure? Of course he did. But how horribly had he failed? She was not even eighteen yet. He could have protected her a little while longer. He had agreed to help Screwtate enlist Treasure's girl Innocence to work in V.I.P. as soon as she turned eighteen. So why did Screwtate offer the job to Treasure? And why now? Was he about to break the child-labor law? And, on top of that, why was Treasure's grandmother so excited about it? Surely she knows the laws and how dangerous the V.I.P. section could be.

He stepped out of his head and asked, "How is he going to hire you, you're only sixteen?"

"Well, they're going to pay me 'off the books' of course. And it's just for the summer so, it'll be cool."

He turned to Treasure's grandmother, "You're okay with this? You understand the risks; how dangerous it is?"

"Well," Mrs. Coalman reasoned, "what's the worst that can happen? She'll get food thrown at her. She may get ordered around and slapped or kicked or

Electrik-Blue 99

bitten but, she'll be okay. I'm sure Treasure can handle whatever abuse that little man can dish out?"

"No!" the Handy-man yelled. "It's worse than that. I've seen what happens in there. I haven't eaten there myself but, in the Blue Room, we get to watch it all. I'm sorry to say that I enjoyed watching it but, I can't imagine Treasure working there and having to endure all of that."

Though he meant well, this was a lie, for he had imagined it. But Treasure asked, "They show Mr. Screwtate's house in the Electrik-Blue Room? That's a shock."

"No, of course not!" The Handy-man scoffed. "What are you talking about?"

"What are *you* talking about?" Treasure and her grandmother asked together.

"I'm talking about the V.I.P. room. That's where you're going to be working right?"

"No! And you can take that garbage to Gehenna!" Mrs. Coalman condemned.

"Then where?" he asked in utter confusion.

Treasure explained, "Mr. Screwtate was walking down the hall and saw me coming out of the unit. When I greeted him, he said that he needed someone like me, someone with manners, to work for him and his wife this summer. His wife's grandson is coming to stay with them for a couple of months, but Lady Kakei has a couple of cosmetic surgeries coming up and she's gonna need help with the little man. He's only a couple of years old, like three. So Mr. Screwtate came in and talked to Grandma' and . . . now, I have a job. I start tomorrow."

"Handy are you okay? You really think I would let my grandbaby work in the V.I.P. room at sixteen? Even if she was eighteen she'd have to fight me to put that skimpy uniform on. But just think, if she works for Mr. Screwtate this summer, and it goes well, he could hook her up with a much better job in the future."

Outwardly, the Handy-man laughed off the misunderstanding. But inwardly, he still worked to sort the matter out in his mind. It seemed very convenient that Mr. Screwtate would run into Treasure in the hallway and then, just happen to offer her a job. Perhaps Screwtate was setting things up to ensure that Treasure would one day come to work for him in Halfway's dark, red room. But that would be a violation of their agreement. The deal was for Treasure's girl Innocence, not for Treasure herself.

The Handy-man decided that he would not let Screwtate get away with this scheme. He would go halfway up the hill to make a deal with Screwtate's boss and, in doing so, keep the vow that he made in his heart to protect the young Treasure. If only it were that simple.

Episode Five

Turn and Run

Determined to meet with Screwtate's boss, the Handy-man began his ascent by first getting past the city agents at the food-court who encouraged him to 'go straight up.' They said this, mainly, so that whatever else they told him would sound correct, especially when the Chain Exchange guard used the same phrase. But they also told him, "If you sense an aroma as you climb, don't worry. It's coming from the hills to the east. Sometimes it blows this way. If you get hungry, you can take the bridge that heads out there. But someone is waiting for you about halfway up this hill. It'd be best if you just kept going straight and get there before it gets too dark. In fact, you might wanna eat here at the food-court before you begin.

That'll hold you over until you get to where you're going."

This was all said to ruin his appetite, just in case the aroma from the hilltop was presented to him as he made the climb. The Handy-man did as they suggested and then, he began his journey. He had not been walking long when he came upon the Chain Exchange gate. When the tall guard who stood there saw that the Handy-man lacked any real hunger for what was served at the very top, he asked, "Are you sure you want to go this way?"

"Of course. Let me pass. I know exactly where I'm headed."

"Do you? And where is that?"

"To speak to Screwtate's boss. Now let me pass."

But the guard informed him, "Screwtate's boss owns a little shack halfway up the hill. But a little higher than that shack is the Boss of Screwtate's boss. The owner of the little shack doesn't really work for him anymore but, still has to answer to him. Why not go all the way to the top of the hill and speak to him?"

"Well, tell me this, since you know so much. Who do I have to speak to about getting those shiny chains? Do you work for the Chain Linked Nation or something?"

"No. They possess the chains only and not the keys. But as you can see, I have the key. If you want those flashy chains you will have to see the owner of the little shack called SOUL FOOLED. But what would you prefer: shiny chains or no chains at all? The one who resides at the very top will completely remove the chain from your right hand and will ultimately remove your chains completely when he returns to the city."

While he spoke these words, the chain on the Handy-man's right hand got a little heavier. But he looked at the guard and asked indignantly, "Be a Free-hand?" He thought, for just a flash of a moment that, perhaps, being a free-hand wouldn't be such a bad idea, especially if his chains were going to carry on feeling as heavy as they did now. But, he continued with his first thought and asked, "Now why in the world would I wanna do that? Besides, I need those new chains to do what I have planned. It won't work without'em."

But the guard reasoned, "When your connector breaks, do you go to the media center and tell them how to fix it? Or do you just let them do what they do best, since they made it and understand it better than you? What I'm saying is, you have these plans of yours, but there's someone who understands you and your situation much better. He can help you."

But the Handy-man told him, "You must not know; when things break, people call me. When something of mine breaks, I fix it myself. And if somebody tries to get over on me, well I've got a fix for that too. Now, let me pass."

The guard then informed him, "No chains on the hill beyond this point." He unlocked the Handy-man's chains and for the first time in twenty-eight years, he felt the freedom of wearing no chains at all. He told the guard, "Wow! I gotta admit, this feels really good. If I didn't have something so important to do, I might take you up on your offer to go all the way up to have these chains permanently removed."

The guard weighed his chains and told him, "You have forty-six hours to return here with proof that you've been to the restaurant at the very top of the hill. If you are found on the hill after that point, you will be arrested. Your chains will be . . ." The guard began speaking louder and louder in order to help his voice travel to where the Handy-man had gone, for he did not stick around to hear the guard's instructions. Instead, he rushed ahead and began climbing the hill.

As the day went on, the Handy-man began to put his climb, his plans and, for that matter, his whole life into perspective. How did he end up here? And, why couldn't he have made this effort to get those shiny chains when he was about ten years younger. The great hill was no laughing matter for a forty-year old man. Far up ahead, to the right of the path he was on, he saw a bridge extending out into the distance. And as he got closer to it, he did begin to smell an unfamiliar scent. But it was nothing that he would classify as an aroma, for it was not sweet; not at all appealing.

As he passed the bridge, he saw a man standing at a table and holding a bowl of cold soup. The man was still wearing both of his chains but, also, he wore several extra chains on his hands as well as chains on his feet, but none of them shining. He also had three unlocked, dingy, grey chains draped across his arms. "Hungry?" the man called out.

"A little," the Handy-man replied as he walked toward the table at the mouth of the bridge.

"Come try some of this. And there's more of it back on the other side of this bridge if you like it."

The Handy-man tasted the soup and immediately spat it out. Not only was it cold but it tasted like an intentional mistake; as if it was poorly prepared on purpose. The man standing on the bridge smiled and informed him, "It's not supposed to taste good. We've learned how to starve our taste-buds here. See, *they're* the problem. It's because we taste and enjoy things . . . that's the reason we have the desires that we have. And our desires lead us to do all sorts of things that are unhealthy. But really, it's the taste-buds that are unhealthy. We're not supposed to enjoy things. Come with me and you can learn how to do without taste, without flavor."

The Handy-man looked at him and pitied him. 'How could anyone live without flavor?' he wondered. He then asked the man, "What are all those chains for? I thought we weren't allowed to have these chains on the hill."

"Well, I am not on the hill, as you can see. I am on the bridge. But where I come from, aside from defeating our taste-buds, we also have added extra chains on ourselves to make sure that we do not do anything unhealthy or harmful to others. And these chains draped across my arms are for you, if you choose to come with me across this bridge to the east."

"I'm sorry," the Handy-man replied, "but what in the world would make a person want to give up flavor and freedom; to put on extra chains and go with you across that bridge?"

The man educated him, "If you were here just two hours ago, you would not have to ask such a question. You would have been stampeded by three men who, like yourself, declined my offer when we first met. But when they got a little further up the hill, they met the lions who live there, always waiting for unsuspecting visitors to happen upon their resting place. All five of the men turned and ran from that place, hoping to find my offer still on the table."

"Wait," the Handy-man interrupted. "Was it three men, or five?"

"Five ran from the lions. Only three made it back to this bridge."

The man from the east made an unpleasant face as he dipped his utensil into his bowl and then swallowed a spoonful of his cold, colorless soup. He reached out to guide the Handy-man onto the bridge but the Handy-man snatched his arm away. He then turned to run back to the road as he spouted, "I'll take my chances with the lions."

"You're not a young man, you know. You sure you wanna risk running for your life against those wild animals?" The man shook his head as he stood, stirring his bowl and returning pity upon the Handy-man. He watched him get smaller and smaller as he got further away from the bridge.

Meanwhile, back in the Nameless City, Treasure showed up for work at Mr. Screwtate's address. Kakei answered the door and did not invite the teen in but, instead, stood there, looking Treasure up and down. Treasure looked back at her but could not take her eyes off of Kakei's head. She was trying to see into Kakei's eyes. However, she could not. Kakei's entire head was covered in bandages as she had just undergone some cosmetic procedure on some part of her face, which had yet to heal. Screwtate came to the door and gently moved Kakei to the side. "I see you two have met," he said. He invited Treasure inside and properly introduced the two of them.

"Her-man should be here with Lil'man soon. I won't be here so the two of you are going to have to get along, Kakei. Don't run her out of here like you did the last girl."

Kakei had a habit of becoming extremely territorial whenever another woman was around. In fact, it was she who convinced Her-man's girlfriend, Lil'man's mother, to leave him in order to go and work in the V.I.P. room just after Khalil, aka Lil'man, was born. Kakei irrationally believed that the young woman had stolen her 'stolen' son's affection away from her, and she wanted it back. Little did she know, then, that it was Screwtate who had manipulated the situation to put this idea into her head. He did this to emotionally scar both his wife and Her-man.

But now, Kakei was on to him. She knew that Screwtate purposely and constantly brought young females into their home in order to infuriate her and remind her of the youthfulness she had lost. And every time, she fed into it. This time, Screwtate was relying on Kakei's fury and jealousy to do more than simply run Treasure away. With just a few artfully aimed words, he could press her buttons and set his trap.

Her-man came by to drop off Khalil. He looked at Treasure and wished her good luck. "My mother can be a bit overbearing. But Khalil will make working here a joy. He's a good kid. I'll see you guys later." When he left, Treasure got down to Khalil's level to introduce herself.

"So, your dad calls you Khalil and your granddad calls you Lil'man. Which name do you like better?"

"Lil'man," the child repeated.

But Kakei corrected her, "Screwtate is not his 'granddad.' Don't let him hear you call him that. You won't be here much longer if he ever does."

"I thought you didn't like me. You seem like you want me gone already. So why are you telling me this?"

"Well, Screwtate obviously has a plan for you. I'd hate to run you out of here before I find out what that plan is. You'll run out of here on your own once it comes to light. And I can wait."

Treasure spent the next couple of hours familiarizing herself with the rules of the Screwtate household: what to do with the mail, who was welcome to stop by and what to do when the media showed up, which rooms she could venture into and which were off limits, and Kakei's daily routine, which included going to the gym and spa several times a week, mani and pedicures, and a weekly visit from a jeweler, whose job it was to clean and polish Kakei's shiny chains.

Treasure quickly realized that she was there for much more than just helping with Khalil. She was Kakei's new personal assistant. And while she had to warm up to Kakei's cold shoulder, she admired the way Kakei was able to live. Whenever they stepped out in public she was always so cavalier and in charge – without a care in the world. However, Treasure noticed that all the cares and concerns returned and could be clearly seen in Kakei's eyes the moment they returned home. There was something that Kakei was looking for which she could not find in or get from Screwtate. And whatever it was, Treasure felt, put the two of them in the same boat.

She worked for Kakei at the Screwtate residence for the next two years. Eventually Kakei softened up toward her as Treasure became a major part of Khalil's young life. Even when the boy was not at Screwtate's home, Her-man would call Treasure to come and spend time with him, since Khalil's mother was not in the picture. They spent a lot of time at the playgrounds. In fact, it was Treasure who taught Khalil to play the popular children's game, '90 and the City'. And it was she who helped him to understand how great his grandmother's husband, Mr. Screwtate, was and how weighty was his name.

Every once in a while Treasure would get together with her old friend Innocence. Spending time with Khalil actually helped her to remember her childhood companion and made her miss Innocence all the more. Sometimes, they would meet up at the playgrounds to watch the children play. Innocence met Khalil and they instantly hit it off. Treasure loved Khalil for this reason, for it seemed that her girl Innocence was much more comfortable whenever he was around. Outside of that, there was not much in common for Treasure and Innocence to share. This was largely because the girls were now eighteen years old and Treasure spent much of her time chasing boys, all the while telling herself that the boys were chasing her. She knew that Innocence would not want her to play this emotionally dangerous game.

Treasure would, however, still share her most risky ideas with Innocence; partly because she knew that Innocence would attempt to talk her out of them. For instance, Treasure had been considering asking Mr. Screwtate if he could get her a job in Halfway's V.I.P. room. Shiny chains were not required to work in V.I.P., only to enjoy its privileges. Treasure did not really want to work in there. But she wholeheartedly believed that if she could just spend enough time behind that red door, then she would be able to thoroughly conduct the investigation she had been dreaming of ever since she was a little girl. But, as always, her girl Innocence talked her out of it.

One unassuming day, while spending time with Khalil, Treasure took him to Halfway's to feed the famished five-year-old. While waiting to get in, she noticed a commotion up ahead of her in the line. It was a discussion that was getting out of hand. Just then, the manager came out of the restaurant to expel the rebel and restore order to his establishment. This man, this manager, must have been a high roller because the chains which bound his hands to his neck where the most extravagant Treasure had ever seen. They were so bright that it was hard to even see the man's face until he moved to an angle where the sun was not radiantly reacting to his shiny shackles. But when he finally did, Treasure was stunned to see that the operator of this Halfway's-house was her old friend, the Handy-man.

She had not seen him in almost two years, since the day before he left to journey up the hill; the day before she went to work for Mr. Screwtate. She assumed that his absence in her life was his way of stepping aside to allow Mr. Screwtate and Kakei to mentor her, since, clearly, they would be much better professional references than even the most famed handy-man could ever be. She also kept her distance from him because she knew that Her-man did not care much for the Handy-man. In fact, he specifically told Treasure that he did not want Khalil to be around him. And so, she felt she was protecting everyone by simply allowing her relationship with the Handy-man to slip silently into the past.

At first, she thought that she would eventually wind up seeing him around the group-home. But two months after she went to work for Kakei and Mr. Screwtate, Treasure and her grandmother were forced to move into another building as the one she had grown up in was purchased by an anonymous investor and then, closed down. It became one of the city's many abandoned buildings and therefore, offered no occasion for her to run into the Handy-man.

She did think of connecting with him every once in a while. But, as often as she did, she remembered the embarrassing moment they shared in the Electrik-Blue Room which they never got to discuss. And so, not knowing what she would say, she chose to say nothing. But now here he was, before her eyes, looking like the very definition of success. He did move a bit slower now. And this was not because of his age but, rather, because of his new chains. Though they gained him more access, they nonetheless made it much harder for him to exercise his will. He was compelled to do what the heavy chains wanted, which was mainly to give in to gravity and press toward the ground.

Excited to see him, Treasure almost forgot about Her-man's rule. She started to wave in order to get the Handy-man's attention but she caught herself. She knew she would have to play it cool since, her connector was set to 'view me' and Her-man was keeping a close eye on his son's wellbeing. In light of this, even as hungry as she and Khalil were, she decided to leave the line and go to another Halfway's. But when she stepped out from the crowd, she drew attention to herself and the Handy-man called out to her. He made his way over and attempted to hug her. She would have hugged him too but their chains got in the way.

"How have you been?" he asked.

"Good. Really good. I see you've definitely come up in the world. I like your new chains."

He looked at her now grown up face and asked, "Where's . . . how's your girl Innocence?"

"Alright I guess. We're not as tight as we used to be."

"And who's this little guy? I guess you're still working for Screwtate?"

"Yeah. I guess you are too now, hunh?"

"Something like that. I'm working for the same person Screwtate is working for; so it's more like I'm working *with* Screwtate. I do what I want here. I don't answer to him. I mean I do but, all he can do is take my answers to his boss and bring me back a response from him. It's a sweet deal. The owner is halfway up the hill. He doesn't come down into the city, ever. So it's like I'm my own boss."

"Okay Handy. All the V.I.P. room you can handle hunh? No more Electrik-Blue Rooms for you."

"No more Blue Room for anyone now! Haven't you heard what I've done? I've taken it to the next level. And I've even got a job I wanna offer you. I can't tell you about it now but you should message me when you've got some time. I'd love to talk to you about it.

Trust me. It's much better than what Screwtate has planned for you, now that you're eighteen."

She did not know what he was referring to. As far as Treasure knew, neither Screwtate nor the Handy-man knew anything about her secret desire to venture behind the dark, red door. But she knew that this was exactly the kind of conversation that Her-man did not want Khalil to hear.

"I don't know Handy. I don't think I'm interested in any of that. But maybe I'll see you around. I've got to go. Excuse me."

She politely stepped backwards until it seemed socially safe to turn her back on her old friend. And as soon as she deemed it so, she turned and ran with the youngster in tow. After a quick jog, she slowed down and told Khalil, "Always listen to your father. Even if it seems like he's the only one saying what he's saying. He knows what he's talking about. Okay?"

She said this mainly to cover herself and to win back Her-man's confidence, just in case her conversation with the Handy-man had caused him any concern. But young Khalil took her words to heart and lived by them from that day forward. If only Treasure would have taken her own advice.

When she arrived to drop Khalil back off at home, Her-man met her at the door and did not welcome her inside as usual. She knew that he had witnessed the chance encounter and so, she began to defend herself.

"Mr. Freeman, I know you saw me talking to the Handy-man but, I can explain."

"You don't need to explain. He was a friend of yours and your grandmother. You haven't seen him in a long time. I didn't expect you to act like you don't know him."

"Then why do you look so upset. I tried to end the conversation as quickly as possible. But he just kept going."

"I know. And I'm glad that he did. I heard a few things in his conversation that I think you need to be very careful about." Her-man paused and turned to his little son. "Khalil you can go head up to your room and play. I'll be up in a minute."

Her-man did not want Khalil to hear him say anything negative about Mr. Screwtate—not yet anyway. However, this was not because he did not want Khalil to know what he thought but, because children often repeat what they hear and volunteer what they know, and Her-man did not want his young

Turn and Run

son to invite Screwtate's wrath simply for echoing his father's words. The youngster hugged Treasure's leg and then headed into the house. Then, Her-man continued.

"Look Treasure, this is the second time I saw you with the Handy-man and both times, he had the same thing on his mind – getting himself into the V.I.P. room and getting you and your girl Innocence to work in there. The first thing he asked you today was what? Where's your girl Innocence, right?"

"But wait, Mr. Freeman, I think you misunderstood him the first time y'all spoke."

"Even if I did misunderstand him back then, I'm sure I understood him just fine today. He finally got those shiny chains he wanted. I don't know how he got'em. He cooked up some kind of deal with Screwtate. And now, he says he's 'got a job' for you."

"Yeah, but I didn't ask him for any job."

"Okay, I hear you Treasure. But for some reason, he thinks that he knows what you want. And here's the crazy thing—he seems to think that he can compete with Screwtate in giving you whatever it is you're after; like he knows what Screwtate has planned for you. But here's what I know: anyone who thinks they know what Screwtate is up to doesn't have a clue. Now I don't know if Screwtate has offered you anything in the time that you've known him. But if, indeed, he really does have something for you, trust me, you don't want it. Cuz it's gonna come with a heavy price. So my advice to you is, 'whatever it is that these two men think they have for you–turn from it; and run from it.'"

"But Mr. Screwtate hasn't offered me anything. He barely says anything to me. I'm Lady Kakei's personal assistant, if anything. But I'm nothing to him."

"Maybe so. But with Screwtate, nothing is as it seems. And since you seem to be destined to deal with two people that I don't trust, I'm going to make today the last time that you spend the day with Khalil. Until you get this situation sorted out and you've got some safe distance between yourself and the designs of these two, you'll have to keep your distance from my son."

"But if Mr. Screwtate is that bad, why do you let Khalil go to his house. I'm definitely no threat to him and yet you're banishing me?"

"Well Treasure, unlike with me when I was small, Screwtate has taken a liking to Khalil. Maybe I'm being naïve and need to take my own advice but, I don't see him ever pulling some kind of scheme to harm my son. Harming you, on the other hand ... like you said, you're 'nothing to him.' He'll harm you without even blinking. And I can't have Khalil around for that."

Treasure had no reply. And it was a good thing because, in the silence, she heard Her-man's words echoing back behind the doorway he was standing in. Her-man heard it too. They both paused and looked at one another with puzzled faces. She was about to ask the obvious question, but his answer came first.

"Oh, your connector is still set to 'view me.' I have the family-connector on in there. This whole conversation is being broadcasted live right inside my house. Good thing there's no one in there to view it," he laughed.

She faked a smile and then looked down with sad eyes as she reached into her handbag to switch her connector out of broadcast mode. And at that precise moment, all the way on the other side of town, Screwtate, who had watched their entire conversation, turned his connector off and went to put the next phase of his plan into action. He jogged upstairs into his bedroom where Kakei pretended to be asleep once she heard him coming. He, too, pretended to have some other business in the room. Then, he sat on the edge of the bottom of the bed and asked, "What do you think of Treasure?"

Kakei pretended not to hear and, equally, within herself, not to care. She had warmed up to Treasure but, this was only because Screwtate had done such a good job of convincing her that he was not interested in the teen and that she was not a threat. But, now, Kakei felt all of her initial fears and insecurities begin to rush back in upon her. Screwtate knew that she was awake. And she knew that he knew it. Still, she did not respond. She thought, perhaps, that by delaying the conversation she could delay the inevitable attack upon her self-esteem. But it came anyway as he continued.

"She has an old friend, a mentor really; they call him the Handy-man. I think he's gonna try to get her and her girl Innocence to work in the V.I.P. room. Innocence doesn't want to. And she doesn't want Treasure to either but, I'm afraid she might be about to abandon her girl Innocence and do it. I can't let that happen to Treasure. I can tell she's good at what she does. So I'm thinking about making her my new personal assistant. You know, kind of like you were years and years ago, back when you were young and beautiful. And who knows, if it works out, there's no telling what she can become. I might even end up taking her to the underground mall with me someday."

This was obviously a hint that Kakei's spot was in jeopardy. She had no idea why Screwtate was giving her this forewarning. But even though she pretended, for the moment, be to be asleep; she was not about to sleep on this new information.

As soon as Screwtate left the room, Kakei got on her connector and sent an instant thought to Treasure: *Hey girl. I need to talk to you tomorrow morning. It's pretty important. Can you be here by 10?*

Treasure agreed, thinking that, perhaps, Kakei might be able to shed some light on things and give her some good, womanly advice. But she had never been more wrong about anything in her young life.

Episode Six

Innocence Lost

By this time in her life, at age eighteen, Treasure had stopped going to her grandmother for advice. Not just because Mrs. Coalman was a bit old-fashioned but, more so because, her conversation had gotten increasingly bizarre as of late. Over the past year, Mrs. Coalman had begun meeting with the agitators from the lines at Halfway's. She was moved by the passionate way they spoke about the hopes of finding an alternative, and more nourishing food source.

The agitators would often leave the line at Halfway's and then, tell those who followed them to meet at an abandoned building somewhere in the city at a set time. And there were many such buildings to choose from. The first time Mrs. Coalman attended one of their meetings, she warned them that, "This better not be about Newman." But the more she listened and continued to attend, the more she began to hope with all of her heart that the meetings would turn out to be about him.

However, the N.I.N.T.E. would not take any chances. They waited with much patience and exercised extreme discernment as to when they should pass around the menu to see which of their new guests were able to enjoy the blessing it brought. And once they determined who was for Newman's table, they invited these individuals to a separate meeting where they would prepare meals together based on the menu and reveal their free hands, if any in the gathering were fortunate enough to have one.

And so, because of Mrs. Coal's strange, new views, rather than trusting her grandmother to advise her, Treasure showed up to Kakei's house at ten o'clock on the dot. Kakei invited her in and was instantly more accommodating than usual. She asked Treasure what her favorite meal was and had it prepared, as her home had its own private Halfway's attached to it. They sat and took their time as they ate their fast-food, halfway enjoying it. And then, like a bloodthirsty surgeon, Kakei made her first incision.

"Why are you hear Treasure?"

"What kind of question is that? I'm here cuz you invited me, genius." Treasure felt the rebellion beginning to kick in. She had not eaten much of her favorite meal but it was enough to encourage a little more audacity than Kakei liked to see. But Kakei's meal helped her to be all the more duplicitous, and so, she pretended well not to mind Treasure's insurrection.

"No silly. I mean, why are you here in my home, hanging around my family; doing all of the little assignments I give you; spending time with Khalil; why did you come to work for us?"

"Well, who wouldn't? You guys have a Halfway's right in your house! How cool is that? Mr. Screwtate has like infinite connections so, if I need a professional reference, I feel like I'm connected now. And plus, you're such a great role model."

"I'm not on the menu Treasure. You don't have to butter me up."

"I'm not. I mean it."

"Whatever. Listen, let me be honest with you. I know what you're looking for. I saw it in your eyes the day I met you. It's that same look we all have."

Instantly, treasure felt that Kakei's words had stripped her bare. She was vulnerable and she hated it. She tried to deflect with, "What are you talking about Lady Kakei?"

"You're looking for *him*. And you're here, trying to prove yourself to Screwtate because you think he can get you in there so that you can find him."

Treasure looked away, wondering if she had been that obvious. She thought that she had masked it much better than that.

"Is that foolish of me?" she asked, hoping that Kakei would not rob her of her hope.

"No girl. There's nothing wrong with that. We all do it in different ways. But I'll tell you this: Screwtate does not want you to find him. And I don't think your friend, the Handy-man, does either. Both of them have been competing to replace *him* in your life. And Screwtate knows that if you get behind that dark, red door, you just might find what you've been searching for this whole time. That's why he's never brought it up to you all this time. I mean, just ask around. Almost every other young girl who's worked around Screwtate has ended up with a job in Halfway's V.I.P. room. So why not you?"

"So you're saying that I should go in there? Work in V.I.P.?"

"What I'm saying is this: you see my life. You see how happy I am out there in the world and how miserable I am when I come into this house. If I could go back and be your age again, I would definitely do whatever I could to find the one you're searching for. But it's too late for me now. I have Screwtate."

"But how am I supposed to find the one I'm looking for just by working in one Halfway's-house?"

"Well, there are two ways you can do it Treasure. First you have to get the job. Then if you're really, really good at it, they'll have you travel around to a number of dark, red rooms all over the city and hopefully, you can find what you're looking for that way."

"What's the other way?"

"The other way—involves your friend the Handyman. He's made a name for himself because of what he did with the Blue Room idea. I'm sure you've seen his handy-work."

"No. I don't think I have. What has he done?"

"Treasure are you serious? Have you never watched the show *Shameless City* on your connector?" The Handy-man created that, and several other shows just like it. He's made tons of money for himself and for Halfway's."

"No. I only heard of those shows. But I heard they're so raunchy that only the most sadistic souls would watch them."

"Well, I'm sure that's what people say in public. But I bet you some of the same ones who are saying that are watching it behind closed doors. But, for most people, he's taken away the shame of having to go down into the Electrik-Blue Room. Now people can view all the V.I.P. action from all around the city, right on their connectors. And they can watch it from anywhere in the city."

"How's that gonna help me though?"

"Well Treasure, think about it. If people have access to all the red rooms all over the city just by viewing it on their connectors, then even if you only work in one Halfway's, all you've gotta do is be good enough to get on camera and then everyone watching will see you. Then, maybe the one you've been looking for will notice you and come find you."

"You really think it'll work Lady Kakei?"

"I do Treasure. But, if you're really gonna work in there, you're gonna have to finally say good-bye to that girl Innocence. I know she's still in your ear but she's just gonna hold you back."

This was perfect advice. Perfect, that is, from Mr. Screwtate's point of view. He knew that once he made Kakei feel threatened, that she would dream up a scheme to make Treasure disappear. He also knew that, whenever a young girl got too close to taking her spot, Kakei's favorite move was to convince the girl to spend an exorbitant amount of time in the one place that Mr. Screwtate had no interest in going—the V.I.P. room. Now that Kakei had done his dirty work for him, the next part of Screwtate's plan was ready to go. He did not have to have one single conversation with Treasure and yet, she was about to end up doing just what he desired her to do.

Treasure sat and thought for several minutes while Kakei went to get ready to leave the house for the day. But when she came back downstairs, the teen was gone. Treasure connected with the Handy-man via instant thought and sent: *Are you at work? I wanna come talk to you but I don't wanna have to stand in that line.*

He replied: *As soon as I see your dot outside I'll come get you and bring you right in.*

She arrived at the Handy-man's Halfway's-house and was escorted directly inside. They sat around a small table and ordered some junk-food as they spoke of things to come. But first, Treasure wanted to know about the recent past. How did the Handy-man get his new chains and just what did he have in mind concerning her employment. And most importantly, what was going on between him and Mr. Screwtate and what did it have to do with her. The Handy-man began to explain himself:

"Well Treasure, remember when you first told me that you were going to work for Screwtate? That night, before I came in to see you and your grandmother, I got an instant thought from him telling me to meet him at your building. When I got there, he told me he was finally ready to grant me my new chains but, I had to leave the next day to go halfway up the hill to get them. But when I got inside and you told me your news about working for him, I thought that maybe he was setting me up. I thought that he wanted me to go up the hill so that he could get me out of the picture; that way, he'd be able to corrupt you and get you to work in the dark, red room.

"So I decided I would go up the hill, not just to get new chains but, to talk to Screwtate's boss. I knew that I had ideas and ways that I could help Halfway's be better at pretending to feed people, like I let it pretend to be feeding me all those years in the Electrik-Blue Room. So, I told Screwtate's boss that if he would grant me new chains then I would give him all of my creativity and ingenuity. I saw how addicted I had become to watching the action from the Blue-Room but, also how embarrassed I was when you saw me being fooled by what was on the screen. So I told him he could make a lot of money if he let me turn the connectors into mini-monitors. The boss, who we call 'the owner,' loved it! But I told him that there was one thing I was gonna need, on top of my new chains. And that one thing, was your guaranteed safety."

"Wow! That's something Handy. But what does any of that have to do with me and my safety?"

"Well, I told the owner that I'd only do it if he would allow you to come halfway up the hill and get new chains too. I didn't want you to be one of those girls with rusty chains who ends up getting abused in the dark, red room. Instead, you can help run things with me. I can teach you everything I know and maybe you'll even end up with your own Halfway's to manage. This way, you'll be safe. That's all I ever wanted was for you to be safe."

"I don't understand Handy. I appreciate that and all but, what made you think I wouldn't be safe? I mean, you talk like I only have two options: either work in management with you or be one of the employees who gets mistreated in the V.I.P. room. You do know I've been working for Mr. Screwtate and Lady Kakei, right? So, clearly, I have other career options, don't I? Or was there already something going on—some discussion about my future between you and Mr. Screwtate—that I don't know about? That's what Her-man seems to think."

The Handy-man hung his head low on the rack of shame which, now, stood towering in his conscience. Should he tell her about the secret deal with Screwtate? How would she look at him? Would she ever trust him again? But what if Screwtate already told her about it? Maybe this was his one chance to confess it before she confronted him. Besides, there was some good intention behind his secret negotiations; this fact might be his one saving grace. He looked Treasure in her eyes and took a chance.

"You know that a couple of years ago, I was hopelessly addicted to the idea of getting behind the dark, red door. I was so consumed with it that I spent all of my time in the Blue Room, pretending that I was the one on the screen with the shiny chains and the privileges that come along with them. Screwtate approached me and offered me a chance to get new chains but he told me that, nobody gets them without giving up something or someone else that they're attached to. He wanted me to groom you and your girl Innocence to go to work for him in the V.I.P. room once you turned eighteen."

"What!?! And you took his offer Handy?"

"No. Well yes. But not really. I mean . . . I told him that I would not sell you out like that. But then he said that he would leave you alone and do the deal for your girl Innocence only. All I had to do was keep her around until you two turned eighteen."

"Why is everyone after my girl Innocence? What did she do?"

"I don't know why Treasure but, there's something special about her. But I can tell you this, I'm pretty sure that if I didn't make that deal, Screwtate would have come after both of you when you were younger and would've broken the child-labor law to get you working in the dark, red room. He does that, I'm sure of it. Even Her-man says so. So I figured, 'hey, making this deal will keep you and her safe until you turn eighteen. Then after that, you guys are grown. If Innocence wants to go work for Screwtate as an adult, that's her business.' So technically, I wouldn't have sold out either of you at that point. You see?"

"I don't know. I guess Handy. But either way, you still get your new chains right? So who were you really looking out for?"

The Handy-man found an even lower rack upon which to hang his shameful head. Treasure then asked, "So, then, how come when we turned eighteen you didn't come looking for Innocence so that you could start buttering her up to go work for Mr. Screwtate in V.I.P.?"

"Well," the Handy-man explained, "that night when you told me that he approached you in the hallway about coming to work for him and his wife, I was sure that he had double-crossed me. He was breaking our deal and going after you instead of your girl Innocence. So I went to his boss and made the deal to keep you safe so Screwtate couldn't come after you. All you've gotta do now is go halfway up the hill to see the owner and you'll come back with shiny chains. You need them to be in management here. Then you can work with me. That'll keep you from ever having to worry about working in that dark, red room. Has Screwtate ever tried to get you to think about going in there?"

Treasure then revealed, "I contacted you today because I was thinking about going to work in the V.I.P. room. Lady Kakei has been encouraging me to do it. Do you think that maybe Screwtate put her up to it?"

"I think there's no question about it. He's behind everything Lady Kakei's been saying to you."

"She told me that I should get rid of my girl Innocence."

"See? I told you I was right. He double-crossed me. He doesn't want Innocence. He wants you! I think you should go up the hill to see Screwtate's boss about those new chains. And, definitely, take your girl Innocence with you. You know how she is. She'll do whatever she has to do to keep you out of trouble."

This gave Treasure an idea. It was for this very reason that she would indeed go halfway up the hill and take her girl Innocence with her but, not in the way that the Handy-man meant. For, Treasure had grown tired of being over-protected by Innocence and was now ready to do something about it. In order to carry out her plans behind the dark, red door, to stand out in the way that Kakei convinced her she needed to, Treasure would need those new, shining, jewel-encrusted-encumbrances from 'the owner.' And she knew that they would not go well with the innocent 'third chain' she wore as a child.

Despite her devious plans, Treasure was touched by the Handy-man's efforts to protect her. His care and concern was almost enough to annihilate the need she felt to carry out her city-wide search in those dark, red rooms—but not quite enough. What the Handy-man did not know was that Treasure was now willing to go to Gehenna and back to find what she was looking for.

And here is the sad part of this entire ordeal. What neither the Handy-man nor Treasure knew was that, the owner of SOUL FOOLED had not honestly made a deal with the Handy-man to keep Treasure safe, for even honesty does not honestly come from him.

Therefore, the truth, that rare gem, must be supplied by another; as I will now provide.

Screwtate, of all people, knew that Innocence was special. But he not only knew *that* she was special; he also knew *why* she was special. For, Screwtate and Innocence, as odd as it may sound to hear it, were once old friends. And being that this was the case, he knew that as long as Innocence was in the picture, he would never be able to do to Treasure as he would like, for she would always prevent it. But Screwtate also knew that Innocence could not do for Treasure any more than Treasure desired. And if she so desired, her girl Innocence would have to leave her alone completely.

Based on this knowledge, Screwtate and the owner of SOUL FOOLED developed a scheme to separate Treasure from her girl Innocence for good. He knew that Treasure had eyes for the dark, red door and a deep desire to begin and end her search for what she had lost in there. In fact, Screwtate had begun working on this plan against Treasure the very day she was born. Truly, he was a very patient individual and his patience was about to pay off.

After several days of trying to convince Treasure not to go, Innocence finally agreed to accompany her on a journey up the great hill. Mrs. Coalman, upon learning that they planned to make the trip, told them, "Keep your nose open for an aroma; a scent in the air. Let me know if you sense anything like that when you come back."

"Grandmom I'm sure there's gonna be a scent in the air. The place we're going is a restaurant. It's the original restaurant that started Halfway's."

"No baby. This scent I'm talking about, if it's real, you'll know it when it hits you. And it won't have nuthin' to do with no Halfway's."

Mrs. Coalman said this based on her meetings with the agitators. But Treasure patronized her with, "Okay grandmom. We'll let you know if we 'smell anything' on our way up the hill." Then Innocence reminded Treasure of something she said she needed to ask her grandmother about.

"Oh yeah, that's right. Grandmom, remember that old coloring nook I had when I was young, the one Handy-man bought me? Have you seen it? I can't find it and I looked everywhere. You didn't leave it did you?"

"No, *I* didn't. *You* left it at the last group-home. That wasn't my responsibility. I told you to pack everything you wanted to take. Matter of fact, I think I remember seeing it somewhere around there while we were moving but, I thought you didn't want it. Figured you had outgrown it, no?"

"Yes. But I don't want it for me. I wanted to give it to Khalil. I know he'd love it. But, never mind now."

She packed up enough junk food to last them the trip, and then, Treasure and her girl Innocence left heading for the food-court at the end of Straight Street. Anyone who was not being sent up the hill by someone with connections in the city had to be escorted by city agents. Luckily for them, Screwtate had made all the necessary arrangements for them to get past the guards.

After passing through the food-court and walking for a little while, the girls came to the Chain Exchange gate and had the usual encounter with the guard who stood there. Even though Treasure did not have many links on the chain connected to her left hand, still, her chains weighed a great deal. "You have twenty-five hours to make it to the restaurant at the very top and back here to this gate," she was told.

Then it was Innocence's turn. Looking slightly embarrassed, she said to Treasure, "While I do this, go on ahead and see if you can smell that aroma your grandmother was talking about. Treasure walked ahead just a little but then, she realized something: Innocence would have to take off her extra-long shirt in order to have her chains removed. In all their years together, this would be her first time seeing her best friend without that baggy external layer; and her first time seeing her chains. She turned back around but, to her surprise, Innocence was already through the gate—her arms, neck and hands finally exposed and her chains already removed.

"That was fast! How'd you get through so quick?"

"I don't know. I just did," Innocence said as she shrugged her shoulders and walked on ahead.

They began climbing the hill and making small talk but, Treasure kept coming back to Innocence's unbelievably swift process at the Chain Exchange gate. She probed asking, "What does it feel like to finally be able to stretch out again?" and "How much time did the guard say you have on the hill?" When Innocence kept responding with, "I don't know," and "I didn't hear him say anything about that," Treasure finally stopped and looked carefully at Innocence's neck. "Let me see your hands," she demanded.

Innocence refused but Treasure wrestled her hands from behind her back and looked at her wrists.

"Innocence, are you a Free-hand!?!"

"Am I what? Why would you think that?"

"Just answer the question."

Innocence thought for a moment about letting Treasure believe that she was a Free-hand. Treasure would certainly protect her secret. Quite a few people in Nameless City had a friend or relative who was a secret Free-hand and, as long as the individual didn't go around waving their free hand in people's faces, their loved-ones would tolerate their closeted connection to Newman. But this would not work. Innocence knew that she would not be able to live with herself if she lied to her friend. Before she could respond, Treasure answered her own question. "No, you don't have marks on your neck and both of your wrists are clear. If you were a Free-hand you would at least have marks on your neck."

She paused and thought for a second while Innocence wondered just how much she would now have to reveal to her friend about why she had been such a 'weirdo' all these years. But Treasure came to a logical conclusion.

"Innocence, are you telling me you're eighteen and you still haven't gotten your chains yet?"

Innocence smiled bashfully and shook her head in the negative, "Nope. Never got any."

"Wow! That's just crazy. I thought everyone got'em by the time they turned twelve or thirteen. I guess you really are a late bloomer. So that's why you wore all those frumpy clothes? You didn't want anyone to see that you didn't get your chains yet. But that's something to be proud about, not embarrassed. You could probably make money telling your story. Maybe what they say is true; you only get chains if you're gonna need'em to limit your ability to damage things or hurt other people. If so, I hope you never need'em and I hope you never get'em."

Innocence felt it was best to let her keep talking. The more talking Treasure did, the less Innocence would have to do and the less she would be tempted to tell a lie and, because of the pressure of that temptation, be further tempted to tell the truth.

The further up the hill they went, the more Innocence began to smile as, more and more, she began to sense that scent—that alluring aroma that she was once so familiar with. With each step, she watched Treasure closely to see whether or not she would become aware of it. But she did not. Or, if in fact she did sense it, she would not give herself to it.

They passed the man standing on the bridge leading to the east hills. He called out for them to come and satisfy their hunger with new things. But neither of them could be bothered by his wares. "You'll be back," he predicted as he stood stirring his stiff bowl of stew. The girls got a little bit higher on the hill and Innocence got a little more giddy as the good air constantly gave her joy. But Treasure was exhausted and needed a break and so, they stopped to rest.

While they sat, they looked up toward the top of the hill. Treasure supposed, "Imagine if we had to go all the way up there. That'd be insane, wouldn't it?"

"Why? What do you think is up there?"

"I don't know. You hear those old stories about Newman. But nobody believes that."

"I do."

"C'mon Innocence, you're already weird enough. Don't go adding that to it," Treasure laughed. But Innocence did not. Instead, she reminded Treasure, "Remember how I used to tell you that you should read the N.I.N.T.E.'s digital book? You never did it did you?"

"No. Are you serious right now Innocence?"

"Yes. What if I told you that what you're searching for in the city is not going to fill you up? What if, instead of filling you up, it's only going to put more holes in your heart and leave you feeling empty? But, what if, there really is someone up at the top of this hill, waiting for us? What if Newman and his father were waiting to receive you and give you true fulfillment?"

"Innocence, I'm not slow. I know that my grandmother's been meeting with those agitators and it sounds like she's been talking to you about it. I know that Halfway's is a horrible place to eat at. But it's all we have in the city. And as far as this hill is concerned, there's nothing higher than where we're going right now. If there is, I don't even think I'd want it. If Newman and his father really still exist and they really have food that's so much better than Halfway's, then why have they been keeping it from us all this time? At least Halfway's has been making an effort to feed us and to make the meals better and better. Don't let my grandmother confuse you with all of that 'mumbo-jumbo about hilltop gumbo,' as they say. Alright?"

At that moment, Treasure got scared because, as she looked at Innocence, the entire countenance and expression on her face changed.

"What's wrong?" Treasure asked. Innocence looked with great terror and commanded, "We've got to go back down." When asked why, Innocence explained, "The air just changed. There was an aroma present. I was waiting for you to sense it but now it's gone. I believe the hilltop will not open to you on this trip. To go any higher will only put you in more danger. C'mon!" She grabbed Treasure's arm and began to pull her up off the ground but Treasure snatched herself away and resumed her climb upward.

"Quit playing Innocence. I'm not going back down yet. I don't know why you came up here but I'm not going to the top of any hill. I'm going to get the new chains that have been fitted for me. You can go back if you want."

Treasure knew that her friend would not go back without her. Innocence watched her carefully from a distance as she trailed behind her, hoping that there was still hope for her. A little higher and Innocence began to pick up an odious scent in the air which smelled like the enemy of all soul's food. This time, however, Treasure responded to the scent as well. She yelled down to her friend who was climbing up after her.

"Hey, I thought you were playing before Innocence. But I think I smell what you smelled earlier."

"No. That's not it."

"I'm hungry. Aren't you hungry?"

"No. Not at all. Not for that."

As they approached the halfway point, they saw the sorry little shack sitting off to the side of the road. Standing in the doorway was an individual who looked as if he had been waiting just for them. He held in his hands two very different sets of chains. The individual held up the more attractive set and then lowered them again. Upon seeing the shimmering shackles, Treasure sped up and began to go down the path leading into SOUL FOOLED. But Innocence caught her arm and cautioned her, "There's still time to go back. You don't have to go there. You don't need those chains. The father at the top of the hill has prepared a more excellent table for those who will dine with his son."

But Treasure looked at her and poorly reasoned, "Now why would I want to go all the way up there when this place is right here." She snatched her arm away from Innocence and went further in. The owner of that poisonous place called out to her, "You must be Treasure."

"Yes. You're the owner?"

"Indeed I am. And who is this you've brought with you?"

"This is my girl Innocence."

The owner paused and looked at her friend. It was a very suspicious look; almost as if the two of them had some undisclosed, unpleasant history. He repeated, "Innocence ay? Well, it seems we have a problem. I was told to prepare a meal for one guest, and now I have two. We'll have to do something about that, won't we?"

Treasure asked, "Are those for me?" as she locked her eyes on the shiny chains in his hands.

"Well, one of these sets of chains is definitely for you: either these shining ones or these which are connected to Curse and Consequence, whom you see here. These are the lions which that liar Newman claimed to be saving people from but I am the one who controls their chains." He motioned with his head to indicate the presence of the beasts crouching down on both sides of the building, seemingly sound asleep.

He asked her, "Most people don't get these shiny chains without giving up something . . . or someone. But, someone in the city made a deal for you to be able to get yours free of charge."

"My friend, the Handy-man."

"Yes, the Handy-man. And yet, it looks like you have something for me anyway?"

"Yes," she said.

"Tell me," he bid her, "Was it harder to carry it up the hill or will it be harder to return to the city without it?" But she did not answer. "Very well then," the owner said, "come in so we can get on with it."

Treasure turned to Innocence and offered, "You don't have to come in here with me. Thank you for making sure I got here safe but I've got it from here."

She knew that this would only motivate Innocence to stick closer by her side. Innocence moved toward her and locked arms with her.

Before following the owner inside, Treasure asked the owner, "What about these lions? Are we supposed to just trust that they won't harm us if we try to come in?"

The owner gave the lion's chains a jingle and they both jumped up, growling and snarling, threatening to attack. That is, until they saw something familiar in the girl Innocence which instantly tamed them. But, as they looked, the lions were confused. It had been such a long time since they had seen Innocence and they had never really seen her look quite like this. They knew that they could still attack Treasure but, Innocence would be different story. And so, the lions decided to wait in order to see what the owner was up to before they made their move on the young Treasure.

Upon seeing them hold their peace, the owner said, "I don't think you'll have any problems from them."

Treasure and Innocence hurried up the stairs but, all the while, Innocence kept whispering to Treasure, "Don't go in. Please don't go in." But this did not dissuade her. Once to the door, they followed the owner into SOUL FOOLED where there were a number of very small tables with no guests seated at any of them; and then, one wooden table that looked like the trunk of an old tree which came up through the floor. It was obvious that this shack had been built around the trunk. But where was the rest of the tree? No matter. Only this one table was set, and this table was set for only one.

"So which one of us is gonna sit down?" Innocence asked Treasure. But the owner answered, "This seat is only for the one who is staying."

"Staying? What does he mean Treasure? Who's staying?"

But she would not answer. In fact, Treasure began to have second thoughts about her plan. She realized, now, how coldblooded she would have to be in order to carry it out. But the owner saw her hesitation and rightly interpreted it. He knew that he would have to push Treasure to push the button in her soul that would permanently delete her girl Innocence.

"Well Innocence," he said, "This seat is for you. Treasure has come here to make an exchange."

"No wait. Maybe I don't want to do this anymore. I changed my mind," Treasure decided.

"It's too late!" he snapped. "Someone has to go and someone has to stay. A deal's a deal. It's a fair exchange."

The owner knew that if Treasure decided to leave with her girl Innocence, she would likely not go to work for him in the V.I.P. room. The only other use he had for her was to feed her to Curse and Consequence in order to destroy her before Innocence or Newman could further influence her to climb higher on the hill. But he was so looking forward to the evil pleasure he would receive from slowly ruining her and the Handy-man back down in the Nameless City. And so, to keep things running on this twisted track, he needed to turn Treasure against Innocence. To accomplish this, he would have to speak that foreign language—the truth.

When Innocence demanded to know, "What 'exchange' is he talking about? Why did you ask me to come here with you Treasure?" The owner cut in, "Stop playing innocent, Innocence. You know why she brought you here. She's trading you for these bejeweled bonds fit for her wrists and neck. She deceived you like you deceived her all these years. Tell me, 'Innocence,' how did you explain to her what happened with you at the Chain Exchange gate? Did you lie or did you actually fight the temptation?"

"Innocence didn't have to lie to me. I figured it out. She didn't get her chains yet. There's nothing wrong with that," Treasured said.

"Oh, is that so? Did she tell you that she won't be getting any chains in the future either? Did she tell you why she has no chains? Or why the food at Halfway's doesn't affect her like it affects everyone else you know in Nameless City? Or, why she knows so much about the top of the hill? Or, how about the lions? Did she tell you about them and how she knew they wouldn't attack her? She's been lying to you your whole life. She never was *your* girl Innocence. She belongs to another and was only loaned to you until you could decide for yourself if you even wanted such a useless thing in your life."

He looked at Treasure and saw that his words were working to hurt and harden her heart. He continued, "Don't be embarrassed girl. You're not the first to be fooled. Many have entertained her type without actually being aware of it. But now you know; it was all lies! So, don't get cold feet now. Return the favor by doing what you came here to do."

Innocence assured her, "I never lied to you Treasure. Everything I ever said to you was completely true and totally for your good."

"Then what is he talking about Innocence?"

"All I can say is that there's more to me than what you know. Just like there's more to the owner than you know about. When I told you to read that digital book by the N.I.N.T.E., I was trying to warn you of these things."

"Look Treasure! She withheld truth from you. That's a lie in my book. If there's one thing I know – it's a lie. And Innocence is guilty! But *I* will tell you the truth. If you want this liar out of your life, all you have to do is walk away from her and tell her that you no longer want any of her help. Tell her you're leaving with my chains and you want her to stay here, and she'll have to do it."

"Is this true?" Treasure asked Innocence.

"Actually," Innocence paused and took a deep breath before she confessed, "it is. You can get rid of me at any time just by refusing my help. But once you do..."

"I know; it's gonna be hard to get you back. But you know what Innocence? I think I'm ready to see who

I'd be without you in my life. So, do me a favor, will you? Stay here and let me go."

Innocence sat down at the tree-trunk-turned-table. Treasure held out her arms in the owner's direction. He smiled an inappropriate smile and placed the dazzling restraints on her dainty wrists and connected them to the new collar which now nestled her neck.

She did not turn back to look at Innocence, for she did not want the image of her disappointed face burned into her memory. But she did care enough to ask the owner, "What are you going to do to her?" But he had lost all of his charm. "None of your business. You can go now."

The owner went and sat across from Innocence at the table for one. At his behest, a rotten piece of fruit grew from the wooden table top. He picked it off the crooked stem and offered it to Innocence, but she turned her face away. The owner then took a bite as he looked into Innocence's eyes, hoping to see something like defeat so that he could finally feel something like victory.

Treasure waited at the door and then asked, "Am I still safe from the lions?" His response came as he turned halfway around to look at her like the nuisance she now was to him. He bothered his self to ask her, "You still here? Go ahead; they're not going to kill you, yet. You've got work to do in the city." He turned back to look at Innocence. Innocence closed her eyes, knowing what was about to happen.

The owner counted the paces as Treasure ran through the door, down the steps and back toward the road. When she made it about halfway, he shouted, "Links!" Suddenly, the lions took off running after Treasure, broadcasting their intentions with their ear-piercing roar. The ground seemed to shake as they returned to it after each leap, getting closer and closer to their prey. One of them, Consequence, swiped at her, knocking her into the other predator. They collided as they attempted to crush her between them while she screamed for her life.

As she screamed, Consequence stopped for a moment to enjoy the sound of her horror and then, attempted to make the same sounds, mocking her distress. Then, Curse bent down and rotated his head in a greedy attempt to fit her whole body into his mouth. He almost had her all the way in until Consequence snatched her back out. Her heart stopped and then began pounding so hard, she felt it would break out of her body. "Recoil!" the owner shouted. The lions lost sight of her as they fought for their food. They sought to relocate her and found her buried beneath them. But before they could capitalize on their discovery, their chains began to retract and pull them back towards the sinful shack.

Treasure got up, bruised and bleeding. She ran while the lions made their final attempts to swipe at her fleeting flesh. Once back to the road, she began to descend the hill as fast as she could. Thankfully, she had escaped them. But that fact had escaped her, for she still sensed the lions and saw them in her mind. The encounter was so powerful that she would not be able to shake the thought of Curse and Consequence from her conscience. She would now run from them until the day that she died.

In her delirium, Treasure missed the spectacle taking place behind her where a burning, bright light shot up from SOUL FOOLED and rocketed into the sky, like a star falling in reverse. The owner screamed in anger and pounded on the warped wood of the truncated tree. He thought that, perhaps, he might be able to injure or, at least, insult Innocence for a while. But, with Treasure now gone, Innocence saw no need to suffer the owner's presence any longer.

Having returned to her privileged point of view, it would be a long time before Innocence would be seen again. And, just like when the lions saw her at SOUL FOOLED, Innocence would look much different the next time anyone would have the privilege of setting their eyes on her.

Episode Seven

Behind the Dark, Red Door

When several weeks had gone by without any word from Treasure, the Handy-man located Mrs. Coalman's dot in his connector and asked if he could come pay her a visit in her new group-home apartment. She invited him over but informed him that she had not seen her granddaughter or her childhood friend. He, nonetheless, stopped by and continued to do so weekly, hoping to find that Treasure had returned or, at least, sent word.

On one particular visit, Mrs. Coalman asked the Handy-man, "Do you believe everything the city says about the hilltop?"

"Of course! Well, I don't know. Why?"

"I'm just thinking," she said, "Treasure went up that hill. And I've heard rumors. Something about someone halfway up who manipulates the chains of two large lions. That's why some people are running around trippin' like they're being chased. And because of them, some people don't make it back from the hill. But, sometimes, the one who lives at the top of the hill rescues people from those lions. Maybe that has something to do with what's happened to Treasure. What do you think?"

All of a sudden, the chain on the Handy-man's right hand got a little heavier. He was already weighed down by his new chains. In fact, it seemed that every time he was served in the V.I.P. room, the chain on his left hand got heavier. But this was only the third time he felt the weight of his other chain increase.

"C'mon Mrs. Coal. Have you been reading that book of the N.I.N.T.E. or something? That sounds a little far-fetched, don't you think? I was there. I went halfway up the hill to the original Halfway's, a place called SOUL FOOLED, and I did see lions but . . ."

The Handy-man stopped and thought. He had almost completely forgotten about the lions. He was easily able to put them out of his mind because his encounter with them was nothing like Treasure's, thanks to a stranger on the hill. After thinking for a second, he recalled, "You know what? There was a bridge leading over to the east hills. A guy was up there talking about people running from the lions and hiding out in the east. I don't know Mrs. Coal, maybe you're right."

And, as it would turn out, she was. Treasure had run to the east seeking refuge from the terrors in her mind. She went all the way across the bridge and, therefore, could not be found when the Chain Exchange guard would have arrested her and returned her to the Nameless City. While in the east, she learned their ways and tried to become accustomed to their meals; to train herself to deny her taste buds and know no desire at all. She also wore their extra chains along with the flashy ones she got from SOUL FOOLED.

But after a couple of months of this, she could no longer bear the restraints nor deny her desire for the full flavor of food. She missed Halfway's because, even though the food of the east also only filled her up halfway, at least at the city's restaurants, she could halfway enjoy what she ingested.

Besides, the East was a chaotic place to live. In Nameless City, you might run into someone who has seen the lions every once in a while. But in the east hills, there were many who had run from Curse and Consequence but not to Newman. And they would, therefore, continue to run. Sometimes, the dreadful memory of those two untamed tyrants would sneak up in their consciences, right in the middle of doing some important activity. At the very least, this would cause a person to flinch violently. But, very often the person would not just flinch but, jump up suddenly and take off running. The memory might even be so strong that a person would quit their job or move entirely to get away from places where they saw the lions. You can imagine how difficult it would be to maintain order, run a business, have a relationship or even a simple conversation in such a place.

On top of all this, Treasure still wanted to carry out her search for what she had been hoping to find for as long as she could remember. And for her, that search would begin and end behind the dark, red door. So, she eventually left the east hills and traveled back across the bridge, fighting through her, justifiably irrational, fear of the lions. She made it to the hill and began her descent. But no sooner than when she began did she have a sighting (in her soul) of those two cruel creatures. She took off running down the hill as fast as she was now able, being encumbered by her extra, eastern chains.

On her way down, she passed a traveler who was being escorted up the hill by a city agent since, this traveler had no favor with the city in order to be exempted from this law. Upon recognizing Treasure, the traveler excitedly called out to her. But Treasure did not respond or even turn to see who it was. She only called out, "Lions! Run!"

When she finally made it back to the Chain Exchange gate, Treasure tried to run pass the guard who stood there but he grabbed her and calmed her down. She felt safe while talking to him and so, for a time, she forgot about her soul's trouble.

"We've been looking for you. When your time was up on the hill we sent for you but couldn't find you. I was hoping those lions didn't get you but, I see now; you went across that bridge. Tell me, do you wish to wear these extra chains?"

"No. It's too much for nothing."

The guard began taking off the extra chains from the east. Treasure was worried that he might take off her new, flashy chains as well. But he did not even try. She walked past the gate and on to the food-court where she reentered the Nameless City. Once there, the first thing she did was to make full use of her fancy, new chains as she rushed to be seated ahead of those who waited in the long line out front.

She did not go into the V.I.P. room just yet. Instead, she sat at one of the small tables and ordered her favorite, foul-flavored meal and consumed it in minutes. Then, she sent an instant thought message to the Handy-man. She included a close-up picture of her face which also showed her new neck collar which looked more like a thick, exotic, necklace. Her message: *So when do I start work?*

The Handy-man was genuinely excited and relieved to hear from Treasure. He feared that he had sent her to her death when she did not return from the great hill. He responded and asked her if she had been to see her grandmother yet. Upon learning that she had not, he suggested that they meet at her apartment. And she agreed.

Their timing was perfect. They arrived at Mrs. Coalman's place at just about the same time. The two of them went inside but did not find Mrs. Coalman there. A digital message left on the family-connector read: *Treasure, if you get back before I return, stay home. I've been waiting for you, but I got too hungry. I finally had to go get something to eat. Be back soon. Love you.*

The Handy-man asked, "Which Halfway's does she normally go to? We can go meet her."

"No. I've been gone for too long. She asked me to stay here until she gets back so that's what I'm going to do."

Treasure sounded like an obedient child, for the moment. But after her typical meal at Halfway's, this type of compliance was likely not coming from a place of parental respect. In reality, she was simply more concerned about ironing out the details of her new job and thought that going to meet with her grandmother, at that moment, would delay her and the Handy-man's progress.

"So," Treasure reasoned, "while we're sitting here waiting, I guess we can talk about the job."

"Okay Treasure. So here's the deal. Now that you have your new chains, I can bring you in to work with me at the management level. You're gonna love how this is gonna work. I got it set up so that you never have to set foot in the V.I.P. room. There's a monitoring room and cameras everywhere. All you have to do is push buttons and order new supplies when needed. And, maybe, you'll need to call in the city agents if someone in the V.I.P. room is getting too abusive with one of the employees or another guest. But hey, it's the V.I.P. room; if someone's getting mistreated in there, they're just doing their job, right?" He laughed.

Treasure faked a smile. This all sounded good and safe but, 'safe' was not going to get her where she felt she needed to be. She was determined to shine in the dark, red, room and, not only in the Handy-man's but, in all of them. Or, at least, in as many of them as it would take for her to find what she had lost in there.

She asked, "The way you see it, will I ever need to go to another Halfway's, maybe to check on their V.I.P. room and learn what they're doing so we can keep up, you know . . . compete?"

"No. There's no need for that. We're not really in competition with them. It only looks that way to the public. If another Halfway's comes up with an idea that we can benefit from, they'll tell us about it and we'll include it in our menu almost immediately. And we do the same thing for them."

"Well, can I go to a couple of them from time to time, just in case one of them is trying to have a competitive edge over the rest of us?"

"How many times do I have to tell you Treasure? No! If they see someone who's high up in my chain sniffing around their business, they're gonna think I don't trust them. And then Halfway's will be divided. And Halfway's cannot stand if it's divided against itself. On the street, our low level employees make it seem like each individual restaurant is against the other. But the higher up you go, you'll realize that that's not how it is at all. Even Screwtate and I had to settle our differences for the sake of the business. Don't go messing that up."

Treasure had to think fast in order to come up with a lie that would secure her ability to travel around to the city's various V.I.P. rooms on official business.

"Look Handy. I didn't want to tell you this but, there's a reason why I want to go to different Halfway's."

"I'm listening."

"Well, remember how you used to stare at the dark, red door, wondering what was going on in there?"

"Yeah. Your grandmother won't let me forget."

"And remember when you spent all your time in the Electrik-Blue Room?"

"Yeah, what about it Treasure?"

"Well, it got me wondering what was so great back there. So I started watching the shows you produced on my connector—*Shameless City* and the other ones." (But she had never really watched any of them.) "And now, I kinda don't just wanna work behind the scenes; I wanna eat there and feel what it's like to mistreat others around the table for myself. I know it takes fancy chains to get in there, but it still costs a lot of money for the top meals. And I don't have it like that yet. But if I can go on official business, I'll be able to eat at different ones without seeming like I'm over using my employee privileges at just one."

He looked at her, quite in shock and asked, "You? But you don't have it in you to be abusive to anyone. Oh, wait a minute. I didn't even notice... where's your girl, Innocence? What did you do?" he laughed.

Treasure put her head down and then, picked it up again as she insisted on an agreement, "Listen Handy, if we're gonna work together, there's gonna be one rule. And if you break it . . . I'm out."

He cued his laughter to stop. "Okay. Everyone else I've hired so far has one. So what's *your* rule?"

"You can never ask me about my girl Innocence again."

"Fair enough. And surprisingly, not an uncommon request. But listen Treasure. Do you know what V.I.P. stands for?"

"No. Very . . . something . . . what?"

"It stands for Various Injurious Passions. There is nothing that happens back there which does not hurt both the employees and the guests who eat there. So be very careful before you decide to go back there. But, trust me, if you think you can stomach it and that you'll actually enjoy it, I'm tellin' you; whatever you wanna do in someone else's dark, red room, you can do it in mine. Don't be embarrassed about me being there. Cuz I won't be. Most times, I'll be busy working on other ideas to improve the whole experience."

Treasure knew that the Handy-man was a dead-end as far as her plans were concerned. But, despite what he said, she was determined to get around. And, after a little while, that is just what she did.

Treasure's grandmother did not return for several days. During which time, the Handy-man met with Treasure at his restaurant and started showing her the ropes of Halfway's and the V.I.P. room. And this education was priceless. They met early one morning and the training lasted about half the day. He began by explaining, "Alright Treasure, listen. There are certain things that you're not supposed to know until you're operating your own Halfway's-house but, I'm gonna tell you now cuz, you might be running one someday. And if you ever do, you'll be ahead of the game. The most important thing here is learning how to liquefy the links."

"What links Handy?"

"Well you know how, sometimes, you'll be eating at a Halfway's and your meal has a . . . like a metallic taste to it?"

"Of course. Those are the restaurants we try to stay away from."

"Right. But you can't really call it because, no matter where you go, depending on who was in charge of melting the links that day, you might still run into that issue."

"What links!?!"

"Alright, you can't tell anyone what I'm about to tell you. You know how, at the end of every week, all of the leftover fast-food in the city is taken through the tunnels underground to Gehenna?"

"Yeah."

"Well, the bins that take the scraps and garbage there don't come back empty. Every time they come back, they're full of broken links; the same kind of links that we have in our chains, except they're all twisted and labeled different things."

"Who's sending them back?"

"We don't know. But I think it's someone from the Chain Linked Nation. I mean, who else would have access to that much metal? All that stuff is either in the Underground Mall or somewhere else underground, beneath the city. But the people who go mining for it under the city usually end up having to make some kind of deal with someone in the Nation in order to bring it up. That's how they get rich. But the miners have no connection to Halfways's; so it's gotta be the Nation."

"Are you telling me that Halfway's has been melting down metal and putting it into our food?"

"Yes, and I know it sounds bad but, listen; if it's done right, it actually tastes pretty good. I don't know where the links are from or what they do to them but, there's something about them that flavors the food. I know what we serve is only halfway satisfying but, the half that we all enjoy . . . that's the links. Without them, it's nothing."

"You said the links are labeled different things. Like what?"

"Well pay attention Treasure, cuz this is what you're gonna have to learn. You don't wanna get this part wrong. Out front, where the small tables are, we call the meals all kinds of silly names to make people order them. But when us operators talk to one another, we call the meals by the links that go into them; and the links tell us what the meals actually produce in the customers. So for instance, out front we might say that a certain soup has flavor so strong that it feels like it bites you back. And we'll call it something fun, like a 'biter-backer'. But, really, the links that go into it are labeled 'back-biter' because they tend to produce gossiping, even amongst the closest friends. Now, take for instance the meal you like to eat here. What's it called?"

"It's called an 'ear popper'."

"And why? Do you remember what the commercial for it said?"

"Of course, Handy. The stew 'makes you feel like you're so high up that your ears will pop'."

"Okay. Well, us operators refer to that meal as the 'ear stopper', and the links that go into it are called 'Rebellion'. Cuz it makes you feel like you're so high up that you don't have to take orders from anyone and you stop listening to those in authority."

"Wow! That's what I been eatin'?"

"Yup. You like passion fruit?"

"Yeah. Why?"

"Well, when you order passion-fruit, you're really ordering 'Discontentment' because that's what the links that go into that dish ultimately produce."

"I'm not sure I wanna hear anymore."

"You've got to now. The only way to go from here is forward. No going back. Now listen. We keep the basic flavors out there for the general public and we only allow them to have one or two at a time. That way, they don't feel too bad about their behavior or start asking too many questions after they eat here. They get to point at the people with the flashy chains and call them the 'really dangerous' ones. And while they judge and accuse the people behind the dark, red door, they sit out front at their tiny tables and continue to eat and excuse their own terrible actions. They actually need the V.I.P. guests in order to make themselves feel better by comparison about their own actions and appetites.

"But for some people, instead of judging V.I.P. members, they begin to envy them. And they start wanting to become one of those guests behind the dark, red door. That's how Halfway's got me. And now, I'm guessing, that's how they got you too."

"So what other flavors, or links do we put into the general public's food? I mean, I know what they're called out front, but what do you call them back here?"

"Well, there's Depression, that's a good one. We've also got links to Anger, Hopelessness, Wishful-thinking, and Pride. Oh, and I almost forgot, there's one called 'Quick-fix.'"

"That's crazy. I'd love to know where they come up with all this stuff?"

The Handy-man took her to a bin in the back of the restaurant filled with small, broken links from various chains. Each link was a different color or had some kind of marking on it to distinguish it.

"This is where we keep most of it," he told her.

"Okay. So what do you do once the shipment of new links arrives?"

"I'm glad you asked. Come with me."

He took her to another part of the restaurant, into a room where there was nothing except a large, rusty kiln and several caldrons varying in size. Then he said, "Remember, when mixing or melting down anything for the general public, you can only put in one or, at the most, two different kinds of links at a time. Let it sit in the kiln until the links have melted into the mixture you've made. Use a metal spoon and stir it until you stop hearing anything clink against your utensil. But if you're mixing for the V.I.P. room, you can put in as many different kinds of links as the customers order from the menu. Any questions?"

"You probably already know the question on my mind. What are the different flavors of the links back in the V.I.P.?"

He smiled and took her to the part of Halfway's where those shiny, broken links were stored.

"You can mix in any of the links from the public room but, back here, we have a wide variety of links for V.I.P. guests only. Now, pay attention to this part. There are certain links that usually go together because that's the way the customers like it. But there are others that *must* go together because they won't work alone."

"Like what?"

"Well, the links for Autonomy and Power normally go together."

"What's the difference?"

"Autonomy is authority over oneself. Power is authority exercised over others."

Treasure nodded her head as she visualized the distinction. "Okay. What are the ones that *must* go together?"

"A good example of that would be . . . Pleasure and Fantasy."

"Why do they have to go together? If someone has pleasure, why do they need Fantasy?"

"Well Treasure, Fantasy allows the customers to imagine all that they must imagine for the meal to taste right."

"Don't you mean, 'All that they *can* imagine'? I mean, it's their fantasy. You can't force them to imagine it one way or another."

"No Treasure. Listen, the Pleasure that we serve back here, in order to enjoy it, you *must* imagine it a certain way. For instance, you must imagine it without the consequences or else it would no longer be pleasurable. So we do not serve Pleasure without lots of links to Fantasy."

"Anything else?" she asked.

"Yes. Here is the most important thing. If you're working out in the general public room, in every dish you serve, you must include a link to Addiction. It does not count as one of the two links they're allowed to have in their meals out there. This keeps the customer coming back, even though the food never satisfies them."

"What about for the customers in the V.I.P. room?"

"Back here, you must include one of the links marked 'Slave' in every dish. But just so you know, the customers back here with their fancy chains are not just here to eat. While they're here, they make the employees eat bowlfuls of Slave soup. And once the employees are under the influence of that insistent ingredient, the customers can do whatever they wish to them: intimidating, humiliating and violating them to no end. So, you might see an employee slipping some Quick-fix links into their meal before they start their shift. It's okay. Sometimes they need that to get through what goes on back here. And, I'm just warning you, sometimes the customers will force-feed Slave soup to one another. That's when it gets extra crazy. You just hope it doesn't happen too often."

Treasure had several questions and so, she put them before him. "Why do we hire people to work back here? What kind of job is this?"

"Well, you know as well as I do that, when people eat out front, they're concerned about the 'after-effects' of the food. Sooner or later, the customer will act on the impulse of the food and if anyone else is around at the time, then that person will probably become the victim of some pretty harsh stuff. But back here in V.I.P., the effect is not delayed at all; it's immediate. And the customers know it; they look forward to it. So we have employees back here so that our V.I.P. guests have instant access to someone upon whom they can act out the immediate influences of their food."

"I've got another question Handy. Which flavor do you like from back here?"

"Well, the one that got me hooked was Acceptance. I don't eat it. I feed it to the employees. Just the thought of people having to accept me no matter what I do, or do to them is . . . I don't know. It just does something for me."

But Treasure had another question, "So, I'm curious. Would you also allow them to feed you Acceptance and mistreat you?"

The Handy-man had never considered doing such a thing and so, he paused to think about it for a moment. But the thought ruined the whole experience for him. To see the workers as people who wanted or needed to be accepted as well was too much for him.

"Hey," he said, "they're just doing their job. And while I'm back here, I'm a paying customer just like everyone else. If they don't like the job, they can quit. No body's forcing them to work here."

The Handy-man himself did not even like the answer he gave. Now, Treasure had even more questions which, he was getting tired of answering.

"Handy, if we know the crazy affects this food has, why are we serving it?"

"Treasure, it's all we have! Newman and his father have horded the good stuff for themselves and the rest is locked up in the underground mall. Screwtate and his boss are going to help us get to it though."

Just then, Treasure saw a flash of the lions. She jumped up and ran from the backroom and hid behind a bin of Quick-fix links. The Handy-man ran after her and looked in amazement as he watched her crouch down and attempt to hide in plain sight. "What is it Treasure? What's going on? Stop playing around. This is serious stuff."

"Shut up! Don't say my name. Get away! You're gonna lead them right to me. Go away!"

He looked and pitied her. Though he had neglected to ask her about her trip up the hill, this outburst gave him a good idea of what she had experienced. He tried to comfort her, "Treasure, there are no lions here. I'm sorry. I didn't know that you were seeing them. But I promise you, they are not here. Please come out."

After a couple of minutes, she did come out. But, to his surprise, she was not embarrassed about what had just happened. For in her mind, the lions were

Behind the Dark, Red Door

very real, and he had best watch out for them as well. The Handy-man pitied her and sought, all the more, to protect her from her fears. But what could he do but try to keep her as far away from the only danger he could see—a job working behind that dark, red door.

He showed Treasure several other things that she would need to know and then encouraged her, "I'm just showing you all this because you're going to be in charge. But you pretty much get to stay in your office and chill. You'll have other people back here actually doing all the work. And, since you've already watched what goes on in V.I.P. on your connector, you pretty much know what to expect on any given day. Even though, you'll have to learn to expect the unexpected."

Just then, she got an instant thought from her grandmother: *Treasure, I saw you coming back into the city but I was on my way out. Let me know that you're safe and hopefully I'll see you tonight when you get home.*

"Who was that?' the Handy-man asked.

"No one. I wanna start tonight," she said.

"Well, your job is basically just monitoring. So you can start right now if you want. You eat for free here so, if you want to go into the general area or, if you think you can handle eating in V.I.P. it's up to you."

"Will you be here Handy?"

"No. I'm going to go work on my next production idea. So, have fun. And don't eat your way to Gehenna in one night," he laughed on his way out the door.

As the night went on, several employees came into the back-office to greet her with, "We've heard so much about you from the Handy-man. We look forward to working for you." She watched male and female employees go into the back and fix up meals while slipping links from the Quick-fix bin into their mixtures. Then, she sat back and turned on the monitor and, for the first time, got a full picture of what went on in the dark, red room.

There was something animalistic about what was happening in that place. The food there was not served on plates or in bowls. Instead, it came oozing out into a long trough, from which each of the customers would dig in, either with utensils or with their hands, and sometimes by sticking their faces into the trench. Everyone's meal poured out together

Behind the Dark, Red Door

so that each person ended up consuming everything that was ordered by the other guests. But they shared more than their menu selections for, at times, they could not tell whether they were tasting something from the restaurant or something that came back up out of one of the others in the room and was then deposited into the trough.

As the meal oozed out, the guests would aim, first, to gorge themselves on Autonomy. This caused them to separate themselves from the others for just a little while. But then, the Power portion kicked in. At this point, they would seek to get closer to individuals whom they would be able to dominate. All of the employees in the room seemed to be having an unofficial competition to see who among them could look the most frightened and miserable as they waited for the rest of the ingredients to kick in and influence the hearts of the customers.

Treasure was already feeling sorry for the employees, but she had not yet seen what would cause her the most distress. Then it began. The customers started grabbing hold of the workers and forcing their heads, face down, into large bowls of Slave soup. They were then insulted and choked with shiny chains and then, had their clothes forcefully ripped from their bodies so that they could be judged, rated, berated, and mistreated in other ways.

The guests then ordered and ate more food because the meals in the V.I.P. room, although more expensive, still, did not even halfway fill up those who ate them. In fact, once the meals were served, half of what came down the trough evaporated before the guests could even pick up their utensils. And the other half that remained only served to make the shiny chains on the left hands of every guest all the more heavy while they dined.

Treasure forced herself to watch. She would have turned it all off, especially when the guests began to do vile things such as vomit up their meals, regretting what they had eaten, but then return just a short time later to their own vomit to consume it again. If you are disgusted by what I have written here, please know that I have spared you the worst of it. But the young Treasure sat and saw it all. She continued to watch because she thought to herself, 'At any moment I may find what I have been looking for.' So, she scanned the scandalous guest-list and would not take her eyes from the screen.

This she did for several months, hoping that she would not have to put the other part of her plan into action. But, alas, she felt that her extravagantly chained hand had been forced. And so, she reached out to Kakei to ask just what she needed to do in order to shine as an employee behind that dark, red door.

Unfortunately though, it was Kakei's aim to hurt her while helping her. She therefore, taught Treasure how to attract more men to her V.I.P. room and how to attract them to herself while in the V.I.P. room, but she did not teach her how to guard and protect herself once she got the attention she desired.

Kakei also warned her not to rely on Quick-fixes when going into the dark, red room. 'Many have gotten hooked on them,' she informed her. But, Kakei said this to injure her. She wanted Treasure to be fully aware of what was happening. For she knew that the experience of the dark, red room was so terrible that, the more sober Treasure was while in there, the more desperately she would depend on Quick-fixes afterwards just to help take her mind off of what she had subjected herself to.

Kakei took an evil pleasure in disposing of Treasure in this way. She was now, once again, the only woman in Screwtate's world. For, she thought to herself, if anyone was going to charm him enough to earn a trip to the underground mall, it would be her, and her alone.

Treasure began finding out exactly what days and times the Handy-man would be working in his Halfway's and when he would be out of the office. Whenever he was gone, she would put on one of the skimpy outfits provided by Halfway's and enter the V.I.P. room, at her own risk. She was a rarity indeed, for very seldom was it that someone with expensive chains actually worked in the dark, red room instead of simply dining there. But her shiny chains did not make her first experience any better than anyone else's. In fact, her chains drew even more attention to her and she was stabbed in the back with a fork the second she entered the room. She screamed from the shock more than from the pain but, before she could complain, a woman who was dining there grabbed Treasures head and forced it into a bowl where the Slave soup simmered. When she came up for air, the crazed woman bit her cheek. Treasure dunked her own head back into the bowl to escape the stranger's teeth. But she could not stay down there forever.

While face-down in the bowl, she told herself that she would endure whatever the malicious mob could dish out, if only she could, from time to time, look through the chaotic crowd to search for what she had been looking for. And that is what she did. When she came up for air, the guests used their spoons to clean her face and, with each spoonful, fed her more Slave soup. Then, the tears began to flow from her eyes. Through her blurry vision, she scanned the room with a pitiful look that seemed to beg for rescue.

One of the guests came close and licked the tears from her face and then proclaimed, "Taste the sadness!" They then began to move her around to different places along their trough and, by their cruel tactics, forced her to cry into their meal. Suddenly, in her mind's eye, she had a sighting of those two lions lying in wait for her. She saw them leap towards her and then strongly reacted. Treasure broke free from the stranger who was holding her and ran right into the arms of another stranger who pretended to comfort her while silently mouthing to the other guests, "This girl is crazy."

As all of this was taking place, the cameras in the dark, red room broadcasted these horrible things out to anyone in Nameless City who desired to witness them. And, sadly, this part of Treasure's plan worked. The word spread, from connector to connector, that there was a new girl with shiny chains being mistreated in the V.I.P. room and, anyone with shiny chains was welcome to join in. And many did.

Episode Eight

Buried Treasure

The Handy-man started getting messages from the other operators of the city's Halfway's-houses, asking who was this new employee with the shiny chains and why he tried to keep her for himself. But he had no idea what they were talking about. He switched his connector over to mind his business and saw the recorded images of a young woman with shiny chains, her face covered in Slave soup.

He immediately sent a message to Treasure asking who this new employee was. And Treasure immediately lied, "It's my girl, Innocence." The Handy-man had been wondering what happened to her. He got excited and sent Treasure the templates and everything she would need to advertise her girl Innocence; only, he did not know that she was not putting Innocence on display, but her very self. He instructed her to set up appointments for her girl Innocence to travel around to the other Halfway's-houses. And, once the schedule was set, the Handy-man himself made a plan to go and see her at one of his favorite dark, red rooms on the other side of the city.

After a couple of nights in V.I.P., Treasure felt she needed a way to erase the memories created in that risqué room. She began eying the Quick-fix bin and eventually gave in to the mediocre medicine. She brewed up a quick bite to eat and slipped some of those silver links into her bowl. As she waited for them to dissolve into her mixture, she hoped toward the great-hill (as most people did when they felt desperate) that this would work. And it did! But then, after only a short while, it did not.

She was rushed right back to her previous state of mind and figured that she ought to have used more links so as to enjoy the oblivion longer. And this is what she did as she brewed up another bowl. Sadly, this produced in her a dependency on Quick-fix links, so that, every day and with every meal, she now had several Quick-fixes. In time, Treasure's grandmother noticed the change in her. She contacted the Handyman and asked if he would be willing to come by for a family meeting to help get to the bottom of what was happening, and he agreed. But, before then, he went to indulge his own addiction.

He knew that Treasure's girl Innocence was scheduled to be featured at his favorite Halfway's and he was on his way to finally see her in the dark, red room. He could have watched her on his connector as she was making her way around the city but, he felt that he had advanced in his addiction past the stage of viewing the action on screen. Instead, he would be there himself, being watched on the screen by others who still had their rusty chains.

He arrived at his favorite place and walked past the Halfway's long lines. He entered the V.I.P. room just as the troughs were beginning to fill with their slimy substance. Quickly, he put in an order for 'Acceptance' to be added to the new employee's Slave soup. Back in the employee lounge, Treasure was waiting for a bowl of bisque that she intended to lace with links of Quick-fixes and share with her co-workers. Her new friends, Shame and Invisible (these workers nick-named themselves after what they felt while working in the V.I.P. room) warned her that this particular dark, red room was more violent than the rest. They then asked Treasure why it was that she called herself 'Innocence.' She informed them that it was not because the red room made her feel so but, because this was what she wished she could be. For it seemed that ever since she was young, everyone always wanted her girl Innocence. So, she hoped this name would make her more attractive to the one she was hoping to find behind the red door. No matter their names, all of the girls had the same look in their eyes, for all of their eyes were looking for the same thing.

They left the employee lounge and entered the dark, red room where they were temporarily safe since, all of the guests had isolated themselves while exercising their autonomy. But they quickly turned to exercise their power over the Halfway's staff. Several of the guests came together and grabbed a male employee and slammed him down in the trough where their meal had been poured. As he lay there, they threatened to injure him if he did not praise them for their physical attributes and intellectual abilities. And even though he had only met one of them before that night, they threatened to injure him still if his praise was not accurately ascribed to match each one of them. When he failed, they struck the employee and caused him to bleed into their common meal, which they continued to consume gladly.

The Handy-man had not yet raised his head to look for Innocence in her shiny chains. He wanted to see her the way she was when he first saw her on his connector—covered in Slave soup. So he waited. When he finally looked up he instantly saw her chains as their shine could not be beaten by the sludge which she was now soaked in. She stood with her eyes closed, waiting, as she normally did, to open them and scan the crowd before she would shut them again while the guests abused her.

The Handy-man went over and began to clear her face with his spoon. "Innocence ay?" he asked sarcastically. But, as he said her name he felt guilty, believing that this was Treasure's girl, Innocence. He remembered that he was part of the reason that she ended up in that room. He thought about the question Treasure put to him about Acceptance and decided he would ask Innocence about it.

"Why are you here girl? I mean, what do you want?"

"Stop talking," another paying customer shouted. "You're taking too long with her. Give her to me if you're not going to abuse her."

The Handy-man turned halfway around and fired his elbow into the man's face. He could not strike him as hard as he would have liked to, for his chains were too tight, and too heavy for that. Still, the man fell to his knees and instantly began nursing his bleeding nose. Some of the other guest who were waiting in a line to see Innocence picked him up and through him down into the Slave soup, forcing him to ingest it. Then they mistreated him as though he were one of the red room employees.

The Handy-man turned to look at the others who were waiting for her and said, "Find someone else." And they each went looking for another employee to attack. He turned back to finish the conversation he had begun. "Tell me," he said, "You're an adult now, making your own decisions. You have shiny chains like me, if you wanted Acceptance, you could afford to order it. You don't have to be employed this way. So, that must mean you're working in here because you want to, right?"

As he spoke, Treasure felt the familiarity in his voice. Slightly disoriented by the Quick-fix in her system, she said softly, "Daddy? You sound like Handy."

But, with her face now halfway clear, he immediately recognized her. He gasped and guessed rightly, "Treasure?"

She opened her eyes and saw the Handy-man staring at her in shock. And she was now ashamed. But to her surprise, he did not address the real issue.

"If you're working in here then who's watching my restaurant right now?" he asked.

She did not care to think about that. And as much as she would have hated talking about it, she wished he would have asked her why she was in the dark, red room allowing herself to be mistreated. Instead of answering him, Treasure ran from the V.I.P. room to collect her things and leave.

The Handy-man turned to approach another employee and began to join in with those who were mistreating her but, within minutes, he finally felt the weight of what had just occurred—Treasure should have been Innocence but Innocence was nowhere in the room. Treasure is the new employee with the shiny chains being mistreated in the dark, red room! And rather than address this he only seemed to care about his business being left untended. He hated himself for this and the chain on his left hand grew heavier that night.

Feeling the callousness of his words, he left Halfway's to go look for Treasure. As he exited and descended the stairs, he saw her fighting her way through the crowd. But she could not get by because of a discussion being conducted by the N.I.N.T.E. Door Jam, Straw-man. Those in the crowd listening to him turned when they recognized Treasure. "It's the girl from the V.I.P. with the shiny chains!" one of them yelled. Straw-man stopped and looked in her direction and saw her being pursued by the Handy-man.

When the two of them looked at Straw-man, they were equally ashamed for they remembered the message about buried treasure that he delivered the last time they saw him. They excused themselves and tried to pass by without being addressed but Straw-man was not the type to keep quiet when something needed to be said.

He began listing the things that those who dine and work in the V.I.P. room suffer from. He cautioned those who were standing in the line not to envy them. "Pay close attention to the drama that always comes along with the lifestyles they lead," he yelled. "It's nowhere near as glamorous as it seems."

As he spoke, both Treasure and the Handy-man felt the weight of the chain on their right hand begin to increase. They came to the end of the line and Treasure would have taken off but the Handy-man grabbed her arm and begged, "Please! Let me at least drive you home and we can talk. Your grandmother wants us to all meet together anyway. Please, just come with me."

She paused and then turned around. Without saying a word she went with him and kept her silence for almost the entire ride. She only addressed him to ask, "So, you were after my girl Innocence all along. Just like everyone else, hunh?" But he did not answer her.

They arrived at the group home and went in to meet with Treasure's grandmother who greeted them at the door wearing a long, flowing house-coat that bunched up around her neck and almost completely covered her hands. Assuming that she was wearing it because she was cold, the Handy-man asked, "Mrs. Coal, How is it living here? How's your maintenance attendant? Anything I can fix while I'm here?"

"No. I got a New Man who fixes things for me now. And I don't think I told you Handy; I don't go by Mrs. Coal no more. My name has been changed to Diamond."

"Is that like a nick-name or something? Aren't you a little too old to be getting a new name? No offense."

"No. A friend of mine told me that he didn't see me as a Coalman. Said that the history surrounding that name, and the things I had done under that name had put so much pressure on me. But now that he's helped me to get out from under all that weight, I should go by Diamond."

"Was this like a counselor or something?"

"Something like that."

She turned to look at Treasure and asked, "What's wrong baby?"

Treasure reasoned, "I don't see how changing your name frees you up from the stuff you did in your past. Call it what you want but if you did it you did it."

"You're right baby. But that's why you need to change more than just your name. The name change was only symbolic. Without the real thing that the symbol points to, the symbol is good for nuthin'."

As she spoke, both Treasure and the Handy-man felt the weight of the chains on their right hand getting heavier. The Handy-man felt he needed to change the subject.

"So, why did you want us to meet together today?"

"Well," she said as she turned towards Treasure and then swiveled her head to gaze at them both, "I wanted to meet because I'm concerned about someone I love. I think that someone I love is addicted to something that is taking their personality away from them. They can't be who they were intended to be and, they're relying on something that is unreliable. They think they're feeding their soul, but really, they're fooling their soul. You know what I mean?"

Both Treasure and the Handy-man looked at one other, as if to say, "She's talking about you." And they were both right, for she was talking about them both. But they could not miss her message for long because, while they insinuated across the room with their eyes, the weight of the chains on their right hand got even heavier as Diamond continued to voice her concerns. And they knew she was aiming her words at their own hearts.

"I don't have time to sit here and be judged, but if you want the addict, you've got him. I'll leave you two to discuss his problem." Treasure got up and left the room. But before she could get far the Handy-man shouted to her, "Speaking of addicts, make sure you order more Quick-fix links tomorrow. I think we're running low and you know how much *certain people* who take *certain jobs* love those links." It shocked him to see that his heart remembered how to be vindictive without the meal from Halfway's, for he was used to blaming the foul food for his bad behavior.

He looked at Diamond and, with his facial muscles, communicated, "I don't know what to do with her." And then with his mouth he communicated, "I've got a big day tomorrow. Maybe we should just let her cool down. I'll talk to her at work and see if we can get to the bottom of this."

The Handy-man left the unit, and then the building. Diamond sat down and pulled out her connector to begin reading. As she did so, Treasure rushed back out of her room to ask her grandmother, "Are you cooking something in here?"

"No. What are you talking about child?"

"You don't smell that Grandma?"

"Oh, I do."

"Where's that coming from? I know that smell. I smelled it before, a long time ago."

"Is it a good smell dear? Cuz if so, I think I know what's going on."

"It's a . . ."

Just as Treasure was getting ready to answer, her connector buzzed with an instant thought message from Kakei: *Hey girl. I've been hearing about your performance behind that dark, red door. I gotta be honest; I didn't think you'd be able to take it after all that time you spent hangin' with your girl Innocence. But I guess you got the hang of it now. How's your search been going? Or are you having so much fun in there that you forgot to even look?"*

Mrs. Coal, or Diamond, as she was now called, tried to re-focus her, "Treasure, you know I hate it when people use their connectors in the middle of a conversation with me. We were talking. Why does that person get priority just because their on a screen. You can check your messages later."

"But grandma, it's from Lady Kakei. Let me go talk to her real quick. I'll be right back." But Treasure did not come back out of her room that night.

The next couple of days were tense at work for Treasure and the Handy-man. They developed a routine to help them dance around the issue. But someone else in the city was also developing a plan to cut in on their dysfunctional dance.

The N.I.N.T.E. Door Jam, known as Straw-man, had searched the city's Halfway's-houses until he found the one operated by the Handy-man. Then, he became a permanent fixture in the line outside that establishment. Every day, the Handy-man would have to pass him as he went in and came back out. And every day the chain attached to his right hand got a little heavier. This made life especially hard for the Handy-man because, as often as he dined in the V.I.P. room, the chain on his left hand also got heavier.

This was not unique to V.I.P. room customers. Even when regular citizens ate in the general public area, the chain on their left hand would get heavier. But it was such an incremental increase that one would hardly ever notice it unless he or she took frequent trips to the Chain Exchange gate to have their chains weighed. In some ways, this was worse than the burden sensed by those who ate in the V.I.P. room; for in that red room, an individual might more quickly become aware of how weighty his problem was and his need to be relieved from it.

But, as for the general public, the weight of their chains grew by such a small amount with each meal, that their muscles had time to adjust and grow along with the change in their chains. However, in the long run, this did not make them stronger, but weaker. That is because the ability to carry around heavier chains is like getting better at being able to carry and spread a deadly pathogen. Or, like a nerve that grows in its ability to be struck without relaying a warning of pain to the brain. It is not because the nerve has gotten better, but because it has become dead to all sense and sensibility. This is how it is with those who have gotten used to ignoring their guilty consciences for only satisfying their soul's hunger halfway.

But, while the Handy-man tried to grow in his ability to ignore Straw-man, Treasure found that she could not help but to slow down as she passed him in order to enjoy the aroma she so strongly sensed in his presence. The aroma reminded her of the first message she ever heard Straw-man give and she wished that she would have taken heed to his words.

Several times, the Handy-man would ask for Treasure, only to be informed by the other employees that, "She's not in here. She's out in the line listening to the discussion." At which point, he would go outside and disrupt the impromptu meeting and order her back inside.

Late one evening, as Treasure was exiting Halfway's, scared and scarred after working in V.I.P., she saw Straw-man leaving the line with a group of people trailing off behind him. She caught up to the crowd and asked one of the participants, "Where's everybody going?"

Looking at her flashy chains, the participant replied, "I can't tell you."

"Why not? I've been listening to him speak for weeks now and I know there's more that he's not telling us because of the city agents and all. But I wanna hear more."

"Yeah? Well the rule is, someone's either gotta give you a menu, or you have to be here when he gives the location. We all have to meet back up there in about an hour. But I can't give it to you."

She looked and saw Straw-man way up ahead of her and knew that she would not catch up to him.

Instead she went home to finally ask her grandmother for help. She arrived at the group-home and was kissed and hugged in the grandmotherly fashion. Then, she asked, "Grandma, can we finish our discussion?"

"What discussion?"

"You know. From a couple of weeks ago. There was an aroma in here and you were about to tell me what it was."

"No, you were about to tell me if the aroma was a good one or a bad one to you."

"Well if it was bad, I wouldn't be calling it an aroma. I'd be calling it a stench or an odor or something like that."

"Well, technically, you called it a 'smell' so . . ."

"Look grandma, what do you know about it?"

Diamond paused then said, "I know I've been waiting for you to bring it back up. And I've been waiting for Newman to send it back down."

"What are you talking about grandma?"

"C'mon Treasure. Don't play dumb. I know you've been listening to Straw-man. And even though he hasn't said the word . . . the name . . . I know you know what he's talkin' about."

"Grandma is he part of the N.I.N.T.E.? Do you believe that Newman is who those people say he is?"

"And if I do?"

"Grandma, I'm not saying that I'd turn you in but, you better be careful. If the wrong person hears you talking like this, it's south-side for you."

Diamond got scared. She was just about to reveal how, on the day Treasure came back from halfway up the great hill, she herself had left on a journey up to the very top, led by the aroma in question. In fact, it was Diamond who spotted Treasure on the hill and called out to her that day. But now, how to advertise the hilltop without jeopardizing those in the city who were connected to it? This was Diamond's dilemma.

"So what's up Grandma? Do Straw-man and the aroma have something to do with Newman? I was thinking about going to the meeting he's having tonight but I don't know if I should and I don't know where it's going to be."

"You know what Treasure? There are people set up to answer your questions in a better way. If you really want to know, let me connect with someone."

Diamond picked up her connector and sent an instant thought asking if the group meeting following that evening's discussion at Halfway's was for level one guests. "Level one" meant that there would be nothing said at the meeting that would incriminate the group leader and, so, it would be safe to invite people who might be spying for the city. After finding out that tonight's gathering would be such a meeting, Diamond asked for the location. She received an instant thought which read: *You don't need to know. It's safer for you if you tell the person you're sending to contact me their self.*

Diamond told Treasure to locate the dot-display-page of Patchman and to work out her own connection. When she did, Patchman asked her: *Do you know the old group homes down on Broadway?*

She responded: *Like the back of my chained hand. But there's three buildings down there; which one?*

The response came: *Contact me when you get in the area and turn your connector to 'view me'. Once you're there and we see that you're alone, we'll give you more information.*

Treasure left to go join with those who followed the strong scent of Straw-man. When she got close she turned her connector to 'view me' and then contacted Patchman and thought: *I'm here. Which building?*

He replied: *Building #154 – unit 3c.*

She went inside and up to the third floor. Once inside, Patchman came out of the back room and announced, "Please switch all connectors out of broadcast mode and place them on the table to my left. We will check them and return them to you at the end of the evening."

She and the other guests did as they were asked. Then Patchman apologized, "I'm sorry that we have to meet in this place. But if you keep coming, you will soon feel more at home in these abandoned buildings than you've ever felt anywhere in the Nameless City. And, if you keep on coming, at some of our later meetings, depending on who shows up, we will even be able to share meals while we're together. And I'm talking about *real* food, not Halfway's." They all laughed—even Treasure.

This became a regular occurrence for her. The Handy-man, however, did not know where she was spending her time as she began to miss whole workdays at his establishment. Her absence meant that he had to be there and that he could not spend as much time working on his special side projects as he would have liked. But soon, he began to suspect that Treasure must be out at another Halfway's working in their V.I.P. room.

He went to check the schedule of the new girl with the shiny chains that everyone wanted to see. He checked for the names Treasure and Innocence but did not see anything. There was, however, an employee who went by the name of Innocent. And when he clicked on her dot-display-page, he saw a girl covered in Slave soup but, she did not have shiny chains so he knew it was not his Treasure.

If, indeed, Treasure had assumed a new name in order to go undetected by him as she worked the V.I.P. rooms, he would have to go searching the city to find her. For there were too many red room employees to check every dot-display-page listed in his connector. But the Handy-man, who always had a fix for those who tried to cross him, quickly came up with a plan to take the V.I.P. room away from Treasure since, he perceived, he could not take Treasure away from the V.I.P. room.

He began to spend much less time at his Halfway's. He labored diligently to get his new project off the ground and, in just a few short weeks, launched his new initiative. His plan was to take the action from the V.I.P. room and introduce it to the streets of Nameless City. He had patched connectors together with mobile meal/media centers. These filming food-trucks were designed to follow people with shiny chains as they traveled the Nameless City offering Slave soup to average citizens. From these trucks, he began broadcasting people being mistreated on the street, right in plain view of the general public.

Most citizens just stood and watched. But there were others who had been insidiously influenced by the media to want to become a part of the action. After years of watching people with shiny chains be treated like royalty and seeing that even the employees who worked in the V.I.P. room could rise in popularity, many average citizens bought into the idea that there was no such thing as infamy; and that any fame at all must be good fame. And so, many stepped up to consume the Sludge and to then be mistreated by people with shiny chains.

The Handy-man's plan actually worked. Once these real life V.I.P. scenarios hit the street, people stopped paying to go behind the dark, red door or even to watch it on their connectors. Everyone wanted to be the star of their own real show on the channel the Handy-man created called *Aimless City*. The food truck could follow anyone at any given time and everyone wanted to be followed. He hoped that once the V.I.P. rooms were empty of customers, Treasure would end her search and no longer feel the need to work behind the dark, red door. But this part of his plan could not work because Treasure was no longer there.

The Handy-man was not alone in his desire to see Treasure leave the other Halfway's and return to the safe role he created for her in his establishment. Or, at least, that's what he was led to believe when Mr. Screwtate contacted him and asked if they could meet. The Handy-man agreed and invited Screwtate to lunch. As they sat and talked, Screwtate began setting a trap for another one of his enemies whom he had been looking for a way to destroy.

"So what's this meeting about Screwtate? I know you don't care about Treasure. Why do you want to help me get her back here?"

"Well, let me just say that I'm sorry for your loss. I know our deal was for Innocence. And when I saw her name on the schedule I thought everything had gone according to plan. But when I found out that it was

Treasure working the red room and not Innocence, that just . . . it's just sad, really."

"Thank you Screwtate, I think. But I don't know if I believe you. I mean, I thought you were coming here to tell me to shut down *Aimless City* because it was taking business away from the V.I.P. room. I didn't expect you to really care about Treasure."

"Well, I don't really. So you're partly right. But if any of the other Halfway's has taken your employee without your consent, they're breaking the rule. A Halfway's-house divided against itself cannot stand. And I won't stand for that! But I'm definitely not here to shut down your *Aimless City*. My boss loves it and I think it's brilliant. I don't care about the V.I.P. money. I think the advertisement we get from letting regular people on the street take part in the action is much better. After being mistreated, how many people will want to travel halfway up the hill to get their own shiny chains so they can come back down and mistreat others?"

"Okay. So then, why are you here?"

"I'm here because, unless you deal with a certain issue, and deal with it soon, I don't know how much longer your *Aimless City* idea is gonna last."

"What's the issue?"

"Well, have you noticed how many people are paying attention to the agitators these days? In fact, I don't know if it's true but, I'm told that some people come to Halfway's just to hear the discussions."

"Yeah, I noticed that some of my customers, even my workers have been giving an ear to them."

"Well it's not really 'them.' It's really only one man who draws that kind of crowd. I believe you know him Handy. They call him Straw-man."

"Yeah, I know him. I don't know how I feel about him. He helped me with Treasure once a couple of years ago."

"Yeah, I don't care. I believe he's part of the N.I.N.T.E. I can't prove it but, I know this much: if you don't silence him, if he keeps speaking against Halfway's and your mobile meal center, you won't have it for much longer. And then what'll happen to your plan to empty the V.I.P. rooms and get Treasure back? Right now, people are proud of doing things publically that they used to have to do in the dark. But Straw-man will bring back people's sense of shame. And everyone will be right back in the dark, red room or watching it on their connector. And Treasure will keep right on looking for what she's been looking for behind the dark, red door."

The Handy-man cut him off with, "What is it? Mrs. Coal keeps saying Treasure is looking for something. Now you're saying it. What is she looking for?"

But Screwtate looked at him and smiled. He then responded, "If you don't know, you're a fool. Now listen, concerning Straw-man, I'm not telling you what to do Handy but, you've got to silence him."

He had waited so long to put this bug in the Handy'man's ear. Screwtate wanted Straw-man dead from the moment he first heard him speak. But he knew that it would be hard to prove him a threat to the city because the people liked him. But Screwtate was a very patient individual whose patience was about to pay off.

Over the next couple of weeks, every time the Handy-man saw Straw-man coming into his line, he would go out and harass him and throw him out of the line. He even got to the point where he began asking people with shiny chains to assault Straw-man since he himself could barely lift his arms anymore because of the weight of his chains. But, to his disappointment, no one would assist him in this.

Buried Treasure

One night, as Straw-man left the food-court followed by those who sought the source of his scent, he told them, "In an hour, we will meet down by the abandoned group homes on Broadway. Leave your connectors on 'view me' and find the dot-display-page of my good friend Patchman. He'll tell you what to do next." Straw-man departed from them but he soon noticed that he was being followed by a group of city agents coming to arrest him. The Handy-man had contacted them with serious allegations that Straw-man was a member of the N.I.N.T.E. trying to start a rebellion.

During this time in Nameless City, anyone could be held in jail on this suspicion. However, this was a very serious charge to level against someone. The trial which resulted from such an accusation was both for the accused as well as the accuser. If the accused person was found to be affiliated with the N.I.N.T.E., the accuser would be rewarded by the city. And, even if the accused person was not affiliated but the accuser had a good reason to suspect him or her, both parties would be cleared and suffer no legal consequences. If, however, the accused person was found to be unaffiliated with the N.I.N.T.E. and the accuser did not have a good reason for suspecting him or her, the accuser would be forced to pay a large sum of money to the accused or else spend the next sixty days in jail.

In the case of Straw-man, the Handy-man did not have any real proof to back up his claim, but he was counting on his connection with Mr. Screwtate to get him off the hook if Straw-man was found to be innocent of the charge.

Before he was confronted by the city agents, Straw-man switched his connector to 'view me'. And, upon witnessing his arrest, Patchman sent word to another member of the N.I.N.T.E. to come and conduct that night's meeting in his stead. Within the hour, the invited guests began to meet back up down by the abandoned homes. One by one, they contacted Patchman for further instruction. He checked out each one of them and then sent back: *Building #152*

As they reached the building, they contacted him again to ask for more details. Patchman viewed them through their connectors and, when he saw that they were not being followed, further directed them. But, he could not have known that they were each indeed being watched, for Screwtate was also using his connector to view the guests who went to meet with the agitators. The Chain Linked Ambassador looked closely at each one who entered the building and, upon noticing one guest in particular, he grinned a grotesquely evil grin. His grin widened into a repulsive smile when he saw the next detail sent by Patchman to those in attendance: *Unit 1F*

Screwtate immediately connected with the Handy-man to ask him: *Does anyone know that it was you who purchased the group-homes on Broadway?*

The Handy-man: *No. When I purchased it I immediately shut it down so I wouldn't have any reason to revisit it or run into certain people who used to live there. But no one knows it was me.*

Screwtate: *Since you purchased it, have you been back there to sort things out?*

The Handy-man: *No I haven't done anything with it since then. I've been waiting for you or one of your people to contact me about buying it to turn it into a Halfway's. Is that what this is about?*

Screwtate cunningly thought and sent back: *Yeah, maybe. I wanted to go by there and take a look at it first. But I remembered you said something about having a certain unit in one of the buildings rigged a certain way. Are those "fixes" of yours still set up or has that all been undone?*

The Handy-man: *You know, that's another reason why I bought it. I don't even halfway remember all the crazy stuff I did in there. I just figured it would be safer and easier to shut it down instead of trying to undo all of that mess. But, as long as the city keeps the power off over there, you shouldn't have any problems. Give me a couple weeks and I'll get by there to deal with the major hazards.*

Screwtate: *Okay sure. By the way . . . I drove by there this evening and saw some miscreants hanging out in front, looking for a way in. You might want to keep an eye on that.*

And the Handy-man: *Thanks. I will. By the way, I don't think we'll have any problems out of Straw-man for a while. I reported him tonight. He'll be in jail for at least a week until his hearing.*

Then Screwtate: *Okay. I'll try to keep him in there a bit longer if I can. Enjoy your week without your 'third chain'.*

Then, Screwtate sent several city agents into building #152. He instructed them not to use the front entrance and, once inside, to flip every switch on every appliance in every unit on the second, third and fourth floors to the "on" position. Once they had

Buried Treasure

done so, he then sent word to have the power-grid servicing the building restored to full power. And then, he waited.

Inside unit 1F, the guests waited for Straw-man's replacement to arrive. Each of them were given candles to hold and light their way since they were not allowed to use their connectors in the meeting. Those who had been to the meetings before shared their opinions with the newcomers concerning, where all of agitator's strange talk was coming from and, where it was all headed. Several of the guests explored the unit to see what had been left there by the former occupants. One guest, in particular, went looking and found an old gadget in a box and was determined to hold on to it. After a little while, a few other people showed up to find, to their delight, that they were not too late.

When Straw-man's replacement for the evening finally arrived, he went into unit 1F and asked Patchman, "Why did you choose this place? I thought we were only supposed to be using abandoned buildings."

Patchman introduced him, "Everyone, this is Steadman. He leads the meetings whenever Straw-man is," he thought about his friend's current incarceration and then completed his sentence, "detained." He then turned to the last-minute leader and asked, "What are you talking about? This place is as abandoned as it gets."

"Maybe this unit is. But this building is lit up like Gehenna. I could see the light halfway across town."

"Steadman are you losing your mind? There's not even any power coming into this old building."

Steadman walked over to open the door of the apartment and asked, "Oh yeah? Then what's this?"

As he stood holding the knob of the open door, he welcomed into the unit the buzzing and humming of all types of gadgets and appliances. All of the guests and, one in particular, looked around wondering how this could be. Patchman walked out of the door and announced, "Well it's your call. You're in charge of tonight. If you want to cancel the meeting, go ahead. I'm out. I'll let you know how bad it looks when I get outside." Steadman shut the door behind Patchman but the humming just kept getting louder. The guests began to look worried. One of them proposed, "Hey! Let's see if the family-connector still works."

Steadman advised, "Uhm . . . you hear that noise? Maybe it'd be safer to turn on a small appliance first."

One of the guests went and turned on a few lights and they each, then, blew out their candles. But the one who was interested in the family-connector did not listen to Steadman. He went behind the large appliance and plugged it in while another guest stood in front and turned it on. The device began to hum and vibrate fiercely; so much, so that it shook the floor of the whole unit.

"C'mon shut it off. That's not why we're here," another guest wined.

Steadman walked over and reached behind the family-connector to unplug it as the screen cracked and sparks began shooting out. He bent down and got his fingers around the power cord but, just before he unplugged it, it turned off and the entire building went pitch-black. The darkness was matched by the loudest silence any of the guests had ever heard as all of the humming all of a sudden ceased. Patchman, who was now halfway up the street, thought and sent a message to Steadman saying: *I think it cool. All the lights just went out.* He turned and continued walking away. But, inside unit 1F, the walls began to shake violently and then, without any other warning, the unit exploded as what seemed like enough solar energy to power the entire city came surging into it.

The upper levels came crashing down to the first floor and everything in unit 1F was sent traveling across the street at the speed of light to become a pile of bricks, bodies and debris.

At that moment, The Handy-man was on his way to building #152 to see about the trespassers Screwtate warned him of just a short while ago. When he got close, he saw the smoke and fire and sent a distress message to the city. He pulled up and saw that it was actually his building burning but could not believe his eyes. Standing there was Patchman, who had come back to see what happened to his friends. Patchman turned around and pointed across the street where, it looked as if, building #152 had spat up a bad meal. "They're trapped under those bricks!" he shouted in horror.

The Handy-man turned and saw something moving in the pile across from them. Patchman ran over and began his attempt to rescue who he could. The Handy-man, also, slowly hurried across the street and began trying to dislodge the bricks but, because of his heavy chains, he could not move many.

He yelled to summon others to come and assist and, then, turned back to scan the rubble for signs of life. And that's when he saw it. He moved closer to make sure that he was seeing correctly; and he was. Atop the pile was an old coloring nook; the same coloring nook he had given as a gift to Treasure when she was just a girl. But he saw, also, a couple of dirty, dainty fingers clasping it. He reached down and tried to lift the large stone covering the rest of the hand but was only able to raise it halfway. But that was just enough for him to see the shiny brace and chain, wrapped around the wrist of that hand.

Instantly, he knew that his building had buried Treasure. And just as instantaneously, he knew that he was too bound to dig this treasure up.

Episode Nine

Drawing Straw

In Nameless City, funerals always took place exactly two weeks after the determined hour of death. And so, Mrs. Coalman, or Diamond as she was now called, would have fourteen days to notify everyone and make all of the final arrangements for her granddaughter's service. She knew that Treasure had been meeting with Straw-man and other agitators, but Treasure was not aware that her grandmother knew this. Diamond thought it would be best to let Treasure tell her when she was ready. However, Straw-man and Patchman kept her up to speed with things concerning her granddaughter.

There was just one thing Diamond wanted to know—how close had Treasure come to considering what they had to say about Newman? Did she believe in his ability to satisfy her hungry soul? Did she ever enjoy the blessing bestowed by the menu or did she die just as hungry as when she was born? Fortunately, in Nameless City, these were not questions that were left unanswered, for those who knew Newman also knew what to look for in order to settle this matter.

At every funeral, sometime during the service, a representative from the Chain Linked Nation, along with the guard from the Chain Exchange gate, would arrive and come to observe the casket of the deceased. The Chain Exchange guard would unlock the chains from around the neck and wrists of the body and then, usually, the representative from the Chain Linked Nation would take the heavy chain that was once connected to the person's right hand. Of course, if the deceased person had traveled to the top of the great hill and dined at Newman's table, there would be no chain on the right hand to take.

But, since very few people were permitted to travel up the hill in recent years, there were many friends of Newman who, nonetheless, still had their heavy chain on their right hand. In these cases, the funeral would turn into a whole other type of event as the representative from the Chain Linked Nation and the Chain Exchange guard would engage in a hostile dispute over the heavy chain of the deceased individual—both of them claiming to have the rights to it. And it was not uncommon, in these cases, for the dispute to turn into a violent brawl in which no one could intervene.

While this may seem a most disrespectful display to behold during the funeral of a loved one, even so, the friends of Newman hoped to see such a dispute at every memorial service they attended. They knew that if the Chain Exchange guard were to leave with the chain of their loved one, then they could expect to see that individual again around Newman's table. Since many of the members of the N.I.N.T.E. had lost loved ones in the group-home blast, together, they looked forward to the upcoming day of funerals and hoped to witness the Chain Exchange guard in action. This was also Diamond's last hope for Treasure.

Diamond busied herself with the arrangements for the funeral. And the Handy-man, for his part, concerned himself with getting rid of the guilt he felt for Treasure's death. How could the building have exploded with no power going into it? And what was

Treasure doing there in the first place? What did any of that have to do with the instant thought conversation he had with Mr. Screwtate earlier that evening? Whose fault was this really, since he would not allow himself to take any of the blame?

He went back across town to his favorite Halfway's-house to talk to some of Treasure's co-workers and friends about her recent absence from his establishment; for surely, he thought, they would have some answers. He went behind the dark, red door and saw it full of guests only, so he went instead to the employee lounge. There he saw Invisible sitting in the corner finishing a bowl of some substance, heavily laced with Quick-fixes. He then questioned her.

"You worked with Treasure right?"

"Treasure? Ain't no treasure in here baby."

"She went by a different name. She called herself Innocence."

"Oh! Yeah, everybody wants that girl Innocence. But she ain't been back here in a couple of weeks."

"Do you know where she's been? Where she's been working?"

"I don't think she's been working the red-room. I think somebody must have put her on the lines or sumthin' cuz every time I see her now, she be outside the restaurant near the discussions. I guess she's doing crowd control or sumthin'. But I ain't seen her in a while."

"The discussions? How about Straw-man? You know him? Is he in the discussions you normally see her around?"

"Yeah, sometimes but, not all the time. Why, he tryna take her from you or something? They say he's a secret Free-hand. I think he got arrested for it though so Treasure should be back to work soon."

"No she won't. She's dead. And I'm startin' to think that hangin' around that agitator is what got her killed."

He left the employee lounge and then went to do some more investigating. Based on her conversation with the Handy-man, Invisible began to spread the rumor that Straw-man was responsible for Treasure's death. Diamond knew that this was not true and so did Mr. Screwtate. And yet, the ambassador from the Chain Linked Nation took this as an opportunity to finish what he put in motion the night of Treasure's death.

Screwtate had originally hoped to quietly kill Straw-man in the building's blast and thought it would be doubly sweet if Treasure died in it as well. However, when he learned that Straw-man would not be in attendance, he decided he would use Treasure's death, and the Handy-man's subsequent guilt as a weapon to destroy Straw-man publically.

Screwtate connected with the Handy-man and thought: *I'm sorry to hear about your loss. I know how much that young girl meant to you.*

The Handy-man: *You don't really care. What do you want?*

Screwtate: *Well, I want you to get back to work on your special project. One food truck is not enough. I want you to equip a fleet of those mobile meal/media centers. But I know you won't be able to do that until you get what you're looking for.*

The Handy-man: *Oh yeah? And what am I looking for?*

Screwtate: *Answers. Justice ... Revenge.*

The Handy-man: *You know something about what happened to Treasure? You connected with me that* *night and I told you that as long as the power was off, that place was safe. Next thing I know, there's power going into the building and now she's dead. If I find out you had anything to do with her death Screwtate, I'll find a way to put an end to your days.*

Screwtate tried to fight back the urge to put the Handy-man in his place. It was part of his plan to allow him to think that the two of them were close to being on the same level now that the Handy-man had those shiny chains and ran his own Halfway's. But Screwtate could not resist the opportunity to condescend. He thought and sent: *You think that one conversation with my boss makes us the same? Or that the only difference between you and me is the number of Halfway's-houses we control? You'd better force yourself to remember just how far apart we are and then use whatever brain power you have left to learn to appreciate that distance!*

The Handy-man's fury mixed with fear as he thought and sent back: *Can you just tell me what you know about that night? The quicker I can get some answers the quicker I can get back to work on my project.*

Once again sensing his superiority, Screwtate sent: *That's better. Now listen. Straw-man was in jail up until last night. Now I didn't feel anything but the agents guarding him said there was something like an earthquake and all of the doors to the cells were flung open. But rather than escaping, Straw-man just stood their rapping or quoting some poem about his soul being satisfied. The agent who heard him decided to put him on house arrest and personally guard him until his trial. So now he's home, relaxing and enjoying the city's protection.*

This much of what Screwtate shared was totally true. The rest, however, was spoken in Screwtate's native tongue, the language of lies. The Handy-man understandably thought and sent: *What does any of that have to do with the night that Treasure died?*

Screwtate replied: *Well, the night Straw-man was arrested, he turned his connecter to "view me" just before the agents took him. He shouted to whoever was watching him, 'They know too much. Don't let them talk. Silence them all before my trial.' Now, Handy, you're a smart man. I'm sure you've figured out by now that Treasure had been meeting with the agitators in abandoned homes around the city. They claimed to be able to help her stop seeing the lions. Treasure was a good girl, even without her girl Innocence. She didn't deserve this.*

The Handy-man wanted him to stop saying her name. But Screwtate continued and concluded: *But she was tormented by those visions. That's the only reason why Treasure fell for their lies. That's why she was meeting with them that night. And Straw-man knew that he had said too much in front of her. He feared that Treasure and the others might testify against him if you brought him to trial as a member of the N.I.N.T.E. That's why he had that building destroyed the other night – to protect his self.*

The Handy-man challenged respectfully: *But no one else knows about the 'fixes' I made to that building. You're the only one that knows how I had that place rigged. And, I'm just thinking, even if Straw-man knew about all that, how could he have gotten the power to come back on that night? He couldn't have known that I was gonna charge him with being affiliated. He would've had to have been planning that explosion before he was even arrested, unless he's got connections in the city like that.*

But Screwtate deceptively reasoned: *Hey, I've heard that there are people out there who can hack into our connectors and set them to 'view me' without us even knowing. My wife's son, Her-man, doesn't like you or me much. From the day he met you he thought you were out to corrupt Treasure. He's thought the same about me. And he's been known to be sympathetic to the agitators. So, maybe he had them spying on us and maybe they viewed that conversation when you told me about your 'fixes'. And, maybe, they chose that apartment because it created a fail-safe option for them in case anything ever happened. Think about it; if they have enough pull or power to make the jail feel like it was shaking and then, somehow, spring all the doors open, what makes you think they can't get a power grid to turn on? I've heard that the N.I.N.T.E. have people working in every area of the city, some with a Free-hand, and some without.*

The Handy-man asked to hear one clear statement of just what it was that Screwtate would have him believe. The Chain Linked Ambassador summed it up: *Straw-man is going to get off free and clear because there is no one who can testify at his trial about his connection to the N.I.N.T.E.; and that is only because he murdered them all, including your precious Treasure. He is responsible for her death.*

The Handy-man knew that his emotions were being manipulated but, it felt good to his conscience to have someone else, besides himself, to blame. By the time he got to his Halfway's-house, the word had already spread that Straw-man was somehow responsible for what happened to those who gathered and died in unit 1F that night.

Now, armed with details from Screwtate, the Handy-man was determined to give Straw-man a public trial on the street before the citizens of Nameless City. He would rally up a crowd and have them march to Straw-man's home in order to bring him to some form of justice. But, to his surprise, when he arrived at the restaurant, Straw-man was already there addressing the crowd and clearing his name.

The Handy-man walked pass him and the city agent who volunteered to turn Straw-man's home into his temporary jail cell. He could tell that this agent had become a fan of the stories Straw-man told and had all but forgotten his allegiance to the city. The Handy-man went up to the top step of the restaurant and turned to address the crowd. He interrupted Straw-man and asked him, "This 'other food' that you're so sure about, where does it come from? Where do you have to go to get it?"

"Well, let's see," Straw-man said as he reminded himself of the N.I.N.T.E.'s rules of engagement for dealing with hostile opponents. He continued, "I've heard several people talking about the hills around the city. Some say there's food in the east hills; others say they've been able to find meals when spending time with people right here in Nameless City. And others say there is food up at the top of the great hill. I'm just a seeker of deeper satisfaction. You know that eating here has never satisfied you. Have you never desired a deeper level of fulfillment?"

"'Deeper fulfillment'? Where do you eat Straw-man? Take us to your table since you never come in here. You pretend to be guessing and only asking questions but, don't you have the answers to these questions? What do you tell people in those abandoned buildings you meet in?"

Straw-man did not respond. He was waiting to see what the Handy-man's real issue was; what angle he was coming from, and so he let him talk.

"These are the questions you would've had to answer at your trial but it doesn't seem like that's gonna matter now does it, since you got rid of all the witnesses? You didn't care if you had to hurt people that we love just as long as you were able to protect your secret."

Straw-man saw where he was going with his line of questioning and so, he decided to put the Handy-man on trial right alongside of himself. He began to build his argument.

"I saw you and that young girl before you got your shiny chains. I saw what she was looking for and I was trying to help her find it. But as close as you were to her, did you never figure it out? You couldn't help her because you were busy helping yourself. You went and got your flashy chains and the best you could do was to talk her into getting them too. And all that did was make her a more attractive target for the abusers in the dark, red room. Have you never stopped to think that your own foul appetite is what consumed her? That's what destroyed her."

"You don't know me Straw-man. You don't know why I did the things I've done. You speak about what goes on in the dark, red room but you don't even know the full story. Suppose I was only doing all the things I did so that I could protect certain people and keep them from getting hurt back there?"

"Maybe that is why you did what you did. But it's possible to do the wrong thing for the right reason, or the right thing for the wrong reason. Neither will stop you from having to give an account someday."

"Give an account to who? Who do I answer to? My boss is halfway up the great hill and he's the one who gave me the permission to do what I've done! Who's giving you your permission Straw-man?"

"Well I'll tell you this much, I've never been up the great hill. But if I was gonna take orders from anyone up there, I wouldn't stop only halfway up."

The Handy-man looked around at the crowd to see if he had pushed Straw-man far enough to be considered affiliated with the N.I.N.T.E. or Newman. But, because Straw-man spoke only hypothetically in favor of the high hill, this could not be counted against him. So the Handy-man continued to draw Straw-man out of his secret societal hiding place.

"How did you get out of jail the other night? Who helped you?"

"Am I on trial Handy-man?"

"Who help you? Answer the question!"

"There was an earthquake and the doors of all the cells opened. I didn't leave when the other prisoners wanted to attack the guard and escape. This man here, Watchman, was the one guarding us. When he saw my response to the situation, he recommended that I be moved to house-arrest to reward my civil obedience."

The guard, Watchman, who stood by his side, shook his head in agreement. But this did not satisfy the Handy-man.

"But who opened the doors? No one else in the city felt an earthquake that night. Only the jail shook. Did Newman or the N.I.N.T.E. help you?"

"If they did, I guess I owe them a 'thank you'. But even if it was them who opened the door, it was Watchman who escorted me out and back to my home, not the N.I.N.T.E. So I guess I owe my thanks to him. And he is definitely not a N.I.N.T.E. member. Oh wait, are you sir?"

He turned to Watchman as if setting up a comic routine the two of them had rehearsed beforehand.

"Not yet," Watchman said in a sarcastic tone that could have been taken either way. And thankfully, for the two of them, the crowd chose to take it as a joke.

Everyone laughed at the idea of a city agent being interested in the N.I.N.T.E. movement. But the Handy-man knew that, while a lot of people liked to hear Straw-man's messages, there were many more people in Nameless City who were looking forward to

Screwtate's plan to bring more of the V.I.P. action to the street level. He knew that if he could frame Straw-man as the main reason why this plan might not get off the ground, that the city would quickly turn on Straw-man and tear him apart. He began working this angle.

"You know, maybe you're right Straw-man. Maybe I was trying to do the wrong thing for the right reason. I had plans to bring the V.I.P. life out to the streets of Nameless City. I was hoping to empty the dark, red room of customers so Treasure would no longer see any point in going back there for whatever you think she was looking for. But, if you had it your way, this new plan of mine would never get off the ground would it?"

"You're a Handy-man. You're known for quick fixes. But I told you; I'm a seeker of deeper satisfaction. Halfway's food only satisfies halfway. What happens in V.I.P. doesn't even do that much! And, on top of not satisfying us, which is bad enough; the food in the V.I.P. actually injures the people who consume it. Your new idea is going to be the worst thing to happen to this city. You would put all these people out here in danger just to save the one person you care about? Isn't that what you're accusing me of, harming others to protect my own interests?"

"But Straw-man, you do understand that this is not just *my* new idea, right? I just happened to have the ability to rig it up and make it work. If I didn't do it, somebody else would have eventually. And the whole city would have responded to them just the way they're responding to me. The people want the V.I.P. action to happen on the streets of Nameless. Don't blame me for giving them what they want."

These words of the Handy-man triggered something in Straw-man's mind. He remembered reading the words of Newman, recorded in *The Book of Trumaine*. In his excitement, Straw-man forgot the N.I.N.T.E.'s rules of engagement and quoted the source of his rebuttal material.

"You say I shouldn't blame you, but Trumaine wrote, 'there's always going to be new, foul foods presented to the city, but you don't want to be the one who's responsible for introducing people to these deadly recipes. That is a sure way to meet the lions!'"

At that moment, the chain on the Handy-man's right hand got so heavy that he could now only lift his arm with the most concentrated effort. But he concentrated enough to raise his hands and block his ears from hearing whatever Straw-man would say next. The Handy-man yelled, "He just mentioned Trumaine! You heard him! That's the guy the city executed years ago for trying to start Newman's rebellion. That's all the proof we need! Straw-man is affiliated with the N.I.N.T.E. They blew up the building on Broadway to hide the truth. That shows what they're capable of. And if you let him live, he'll probably do the same thing to my plans to bring the V.I.P. life out on to the streets of the city. This man is good for Gehenna and not far from the flames! If you love Nameless City, let his flesh feed the fires just like his friend Trumaine!"

Screwtate, who was watching the action via his connector, had sent a squad of city agents to the scene to pretend to be about keeping the peace. But, once Straw-man revealed his allegiance to Newman, Screwtate smiled and ordered the agents to incite the crowd to capitally punish him. Then, the massive mob began to lay hands on Straw-man.

At first, Watchman tried to protect him. "This man is under the city's protection. If you lay hands on him you are raising a fist against the city," he shouted. Watchman was an imposing figure, the site of his stature and strength made the crowd slow to attack. But, upon seeing the battalion of city agents questioning his actions with their twisted up faces, Watchman quickly, though regretfully, stepped away from his detainee. "I'm responsible for him," he shouted, "He's my prisoner." But his co-workers refuted, "Check your connector. We just got orders. Plus you heard what this man just said about Trumaine." Watchman had indeed heard what Straw-man said. But this was not the first time.

During the assault on Straw-man, the Handy-man could not participate, for the weight of his chains would not allow him to. Instead, he stayed back to watch the belongings and hold the coats of those who attacked the agitator. They carried Straw-man off toward Gehenna and he would not see the city again until its name changed and the great hill grew down into a gross hole.

Watchman followed the blood craving crowd through what used to be the woods and looked on as they presented Straw-man to the flames. He watched closely, hoping to see something of the stories he had heard about Newman and that ghastly place. He even hoped toward the high hill that someone would come down to intervene. Then, he made vows of what he would do if, indeed, someone did come to the rescue. And when his vow did not prevent the death of his friend, he made another vow.

Later that night, Screwtate sent word to the Handy-man: *Good Job. You're finally free from your third chain. Are you ready to get back to work?*

The Handy-man: *Almost. But that's not enough.*

Screwtate: *What do you mean?*

The Handy-man: *Straw-man wasn't working alone. You said he had help getting out of jail. He sent a message to someone just before he got arrested. Can you tell me who? Get me a list of everyone he's been communicating with and get me a warrant for their arrest. I'll bring them in to the city and prosecute them just like I did Straw-man.*

Screwtate laughed and then sent: *I like your zeal. But I don't care about any of that right now. I need you to get those food trucks out on the road feeding and filming the citizens of Nameless City. If you're so passionate about tracking down the N.I.N.T.E., I'll get you the warrants. But you'll have to do that on your own time. You hear me?*

The Handy-man: *Yeah. I gotchu.*

The Handy-man spent the next four days working on this special project for the Chain Linked Ambassador. He was, however, unable to work with much enthusiasm now that he no longer needed to take red room customers away from Treasure. But he knew that he would be in the deepest of trouble if he disappointed Mr. Screwtate. Once he was satisfied with the mobile meal/media center fleet of food trucks, he sent a message to the Ambassador letting him know that the vehicles were ready and asking if the warrants to arrest the N.I.N.E.T.E. affiliates had been processed.

While he waited for a reply, he decided to go to Halfway's and make himself a meal. He looked over the menu and found what he thought he needed - a cold dish which, out front, was called 'Just-ice.' This was a play on the word 'justice' and those who enjoyed it always felt more concerned about social issues and righting the wrongs in their vicinity shortly after consuming it. But their efforts often failed miserably and met with disastrous results, only making matters worse. This is because, in the back of the restaurant, the operators knew that the links melted into the meal were not sent back from

Gehenna with the word 'justice' on the bin, but with 'vengeance.' And the two are not the same.

After eating, he still had not heard back from Screwtate so he decided to go and meet with Diamond to inform her of his plans to exact revenge on the N.I.N.T.E. She, again, came to the door in an oversized, flowing housecoat, even though it was warm in the apartment. This caused the Handy-man to pity her as he assumed she was having a hard time keeping warm in her old age. "I've got some good news to tell you," he said. But he noticed that she did not light up at his preliminary announcement. "What's wrong?" he asked.

"It's nothing for you to worry about Handy."

"Nothing? C'mon Mrs. Coal. You can tell me."

"Diamond," she corrected him.

"I'm sorry. Diamond. What's wrong?"

"I'm just tired. Sad and tired."

"'Cause of Treasure. I know."

"No. Not just Treasure. I'm sitting here preparing for her funeral and then, just the other day, I lost another close friend of mine."

"I'm sorry. Was it anybody that I know?"

She looked at him, wanting him to know what he could not.

"What's your news Handy?"

"Well. I know you've been busy preparing for the funeral. But I don't want you to think that I've forgotten about her. I've been out looking for the people who did this to her."

"What are you talking about Handy?"

"Mrs. Co . . . Diamond. This was no accident. Treasure was meeting with those agitators after the discussions down at Halfway's. But they're all N.I.N.T.E. members. One of the main ones, a guy named Straw-man got arrested the other night and, before the agents took him, he gave the order for his friends to blow up the building they were meeting in so that no one could testify about his affiliation. I put him on trial and the public found him guilty right on the street. He paid for it Mrs. Coal. I'm mean, Diamond. He paid for what he did!"

"Did he admit to all that Handy?"

"Of course not. But he revealed his connection to Newman. I got him to do it. That's what did him in."

"So now what Handy?"

"So now what? So now I'm gonna get warrants to go and arrest the others who are tied to Straw-man. I'm going to bring them in to the city and prosecute their whole movement, bit by bit. They're all good for Gehenna."

"And what will you do to yourself for the role you played in her death Handy?"

"What? What do you mean?"

"You're putting the wrong people on trial. Newman and the N.I.N.T.E. are not responsible for this. They were only trying to help. I told you, back when Treasure was only thirteen years old, that you were the one who needed to help her because you were the one who sent her down this road."

"You said that, and you keep saying it. But you never told me what you mean. Treasure's not here anymore so she can't do it. So won't you, finally, tell me what you're talking about?"

"Don't you remember Handy, when she was just a child; that night when you and I were angry with one another? You were the one who carelessly informed Treasure that her father left to go spend all his time in the V.I.P. room. From that day forward, she never looked at that door the same. She wanted to go in there and look for him. Her girl Innocence tried to keep her out of there. I even invited you to do for her what her father should have done—show her that she was more important than what was behind that door."

The Handy-man began to think of all the opportunities he had missed to play this important role in the young girl's life. He thought of the few occasions when he did try hard, but mostly of how selfish he had been.

Diamond continued, "I thought that you two could help each other Handy; that you would stop looking to get behind that door once you saw the way she was beginning to look at it and instead, focus on being a father figure to her. But the more you looked at that door, the more convinced she became that what she was looking for must be back there. She thought that if she was one of those employees working back there, then maybe her father, or you, would look at her the way you looked at that door."

As Diamond spoke, the weight of the chains on both of the Handy-man's wrists became unbearable. He dropped and sunk like a sandbag into the couch behind him, unable to rise under the weight of his guilt.

But she continued. "And when Treasure got older Handy, you were the one who sent her up the hill, not to Newman but, only halfway where she saw those lions. You were the one who taught her how to prepare what is served in that dark, red room. You told her to schedule the one, who you thought was Innocence, to work all over town. And Handy, I've gotta say, you were the one who spent all his time eating that which made the chain on your left hand so heavy. And, by ignoring everything that was said to you about Newman, you increased the weight of the chain on your right hand too. So, ultimately, it was because of all of this that you were unable to lift a finger to rescue my buried Treasure."

But he responded in anger, "Stop it! Stop saying these things! I never wanted her to work in that place. I thought I could send her girl Innocence in there instead."

"No Handy! Treasure told you and I told you; you can't get one without the other. Now with your lips, you may have told her to keep Innocence around; but by your actions and your addiction to that dark door, you convinced her that she would be better off, more important to you and to men in general without Innocence."

Drawing Straw 255

He wanted to lift his hands to cover his ears but could only lift his left arm; and that, only a little. He screamed, "Why is this chain so heavy? Every time somebody says something about that hill or Newman, this one gets worse. Why would he do that to me? It's Newman's fault that I couldn't unbury Treasury!"

"No Handy. The weight of that chain is not meant to make your life miserable. It's meant to motivate you to seek to have the chain removed. But you would not be persuaded to do so."

At that moment, the very idea of having the heavy chain on his right hand removed brought to his mind the most meaningful concept of hope he had ever held. He remembered the advice the Chain Exchange guard gave him about traveling to the top of the hill to be forever freed from his fetter. The Handy-man looked around and asked Diamond, "What's going on? Are you cooking something in here?" as the aroma of soul's food danced around the apartment.

Diamond responded, "Oh I'm cooking something alright. But if you want any more than what you're sensing right now, you're gonna have to go back up the hill, twice as far as you went last time. Listen Handy. I hear what you're planning to do to the N.I.N.T.E. But you need to abandon that plan. I don't know why that old group-home collapsed the way it did, but I know Newman did not do it. And neither did the N.I.N.T.E. They only sought to relieve Treasure of her heavy chain and set her free from her fear of the lions. You're gonna have to look for someone else to blame for her death. And I don't know who that is."

He thought for a sober moment and then started to reply with, "I do." It was time for him to confess how he had rigged the apartment building all those years ago. He would tell her of the role he played in Treasure's death and seek her forgiveness. But just as he was about to utter the first words of his confession, his connector buzzed with an instant thought from Mr. Screwtate. Suddenly, the Aroma was gone and his chains felt lighter again. Whatever had happened in that moment had passed and the Handy-man swallowed the admission he was about to make.

He wiped his eyes which had teared up and then excused his self while he stepped out to read the message which said: *I have the warrants. I'm sending them to your connector now. As soon as you get within five feet of one of the individuals on this list, the warrant will be sent to their connector to confirm your right to arrest them. The list contains the names of all suspected affiliates.*

The Handy-man did not yet look at the list. He went back inside the apartment, having forgotten about the aroma he sensed just moments before. As he walked over to sit down again, Diamonds connector beeped with a strange sounding alert. The Handy-man's connector also beeped, sounding more like a tracking or honing device. He looked at his old friend, quite suspiciously now. "Diamond," he said slowly, now much more conscious of her previous pro-Newman remarks, "who was the friend that you said passed away a couple of days ago?"

"His name was Stroughman."

"And who did you say it was that gave you your new name?"

"I didn't say."

"Why have you been wearing that housecoat every time I come over? It's not cold in here. And didn't you say you had a *new man* fixing things for you?"

"What are you trying to say Handy?"

"Can I see your wrists Mrs. Coalman; particularly your right wrist?"

"You know the law Handy. If you're working for the city, which I assume you are, you can't come into someone's house and ask them to show you their wrist without a warrant. And if you're in my house with a warrant that you didn't tell me about, your warrant is no good."

"Mrs. Coal, why do you know so much about warrants all of a sudden?"

"My name is Diamond now, Handy. Newman calls me Diamond."

She looked at him, her eyes daring him to act on the warrant that she knew he had. The dare was not based on her knowledge of the law but, rather, on the strength of their relationship that she, once again, was willing to trust to be stronger than anything Halfway's could produce.

He turned halfway around, unwilling to look her in the eyes, and said, "Mrs. Coal, I have a list of suspected traitors. I'm going to go arrest everyone whose name is on this list. And then, after Treasure's funeral, you and I are going to finish this conversation." He walked quickly to the door and let himself out, hoping that Screwtate was not aware that he had just left the apartment of one of the suspects on the list without making an arrest.

After he closed her door, Diamond rushed over and locked it behind him, then she spoke to Newman in her heart, asking him to send the Aroma to draw the Handy-man to the great hill; to do something, anything to rescue her friends from the Handy-man and, also, to rescue the Handy-man from himself and from Newman's lions.

As soon as her heart finished making these requests, she heard disturbing noises coming from just outside, in front of her building. She ran to the window and looked, but could not see what was causing the commotion. But, Diamond was sure that she knew exactly who it was. And she was right.

Episode Ten

Under Arrest

Leaving Diamond's home, the Handy-man was met by a squad of city agents who came to assist him in serving the arrest warrants. Patchman, whose name was first on the list, lived right around the corner from Diamond. The Handy-man tried to lead the agents there first, but one of them said, "Wait, doesn't one of them live here?" But he redirected, "No I just checked, it was an old woman and they say she moved to another home. I'll worry about her later. I think they're ranked in order of importance so let's work our way down the list."

They headed off to Patchman's but before they could turn the corner, suddenly, several startling things happened all at once. If you were to ask those who were there, you would hear several different stories about what actually occurred. But, were you to ask the Handy-man, this is what you would likely hear.

First, a bright light flashed which did challenge and defeat the vision of most of the men traveling with him. The Handy-man tried to lift his hands to shield his eyes but he could not raise them any higher than his own shoulders. He tucked his head to bury his face into his raised hands but, very soon, he would drop them because of the weight of his chains. The few city agents who were not permitted to see the blinding light looked around trying to figure out what was happening to the others who stumbled around, trying to feel for a point of reference. Then, a deafening voice penetrated the air and beat upon the eardrums of the agents who were still standing.

The agents who were blinded by the light did not hear the voice. They, instead, only heard their friends screaming, "My ears!" and wondered why they were not shouting, "My eyes!" Yet, while the Handy-man's eyes and ears were confronted as well, he saw and heard more clearly than he ever had before, for all he saw was light and all he heard was truth. The deafening voice which opened his ears asked, "You are a Handy-man? Why are you breaking all of my things?"

"What things? Who are you?"

"You violate my health codes; you ruin people's appetite to satisfy your own greed; you crave vindication for yourself, even though you vindictively spew venom at all of your enemies; and now you are out to prosecute me."

"How? Who are you?"

The Handyman assumed that the one speaking to him was the suspected member of the N.I.N.T.E. whose home was just down the street. In his confusion, he could not quite remember the name from his list and so he asked, "Tell me your name?"

"My name is illegal in this city. Are you sure you want me to say it?"

The Handy-man thought for a moment about what was happening to him as he put the pieces together. "Wait," he said to the Light Bearer. "You shook the jail for Straw-man?"

"I did."

"You're not Patchman."

"No."

"Your name is not on my list."

"No."

"Your name is the reason for my list."

"Yes."

At that moment, the aroma of soul's food returned and wrapped the Handy-man in an aura so powerfully pleasant that he began to cry when it left him. He said, softly as he lifted his head, "You're Newman."

"Yes, I'm Newman and with your arrest warrants, you are on your way to throw me into Gehenna, bit by bit."

When he said this, the bright light revealed the most glorious face shining forth at its core. This face was full of beauty and grace, and yet, there was something of displeasure in the countenance. But as the Handy-man looked on, he realized that he had seen this kind face once before, when he was halfway up the hill. He recalled how, after making the deal with the owner of SOUL FOOLED, he was allowed to enter the cash-n-carry room which contained stolen items from the underground mall. He got his shiny chains and thanked the owner. But as he was leaving, the lions somehow got loose. Those new chains, which the Handy-man was so glad to receive, instantly proved to be a burden, weighing him down and preventing him from fleeing fast enough to save his life.

As he ran, he called for the owner's help but there did not seem to be any response from him. Thankfully, just before the lions reached him, someone stepped in and fought the lions for him, forcing them back. As he escaped, the Handy-man turned halfway around to see the one who was wounded to save him but, he did not stay to thank the man. He only ran away, back to the road. The Handy-man was afraid that if he stayed in that place one second longer, he would develop that irrational fear of those fierce felines harassing him forever.

He quickly forgot about the encounter as he descended the hill. Astonished by how much faster he was now able to travel, he gave his new chains the credit. In his mind, this was proof of how much easier his life was going to be because of them. What he should have concluded, however, was that the weight of his chains was bringing him down faster and would make traveling back up the hill all the more difficult, should he ever desire to do so again.

But now, as he looked on and saw Newman in this new light, he slowly began to understand what great gratitude he owed him for rescuing him that day. He wanted to thank him but, the light illuminating Newman's face began to grow dim. Now he saw Newman standing, hunched over, and weighed down while wearing something that clearly did not belong to him. As he looked closer, he saw that Newman was wearing the Handy-man's heavy chain. And in that moment, the Handy-man's right hand, all of a sudden, felt free and as light as a feather. He started to lift his hand and rejoice at his liberation but, he did not. For, when he saw the awful misery that his chain put upon Newman, he was very sorrowful and ashamed.

Suddenly, the scene began to brighten as the face of Newman flashed a most benevolent smile before returning to pure light. This light blinded the Handy-man who desperately wished to regain his sight; not for any other reason than to see Newman's smile again, for he desperately wanted to know whether or not Newman was still wearing his heavy chain as his own right hand still felt very free. He now only heard the voice say to him, "Leave these men. Go from here to the foot of the west hills and find my friend Bro-man. He will restore your sight and tell you how, even with the weight of your heavy chains, you may still lift up my name."

The voice left and so did the light. The Handy-man noticed that his right hand was once again weighed down by his chain but, now, it was not even half as heavy as it had been. It was, in fact, twice as light. He wholeheartedly believed that this vision, this epiphany, was Newman's vow to somehow, someday, take that burdensome chain away from him completely and make him a Free-hand. With this hope, the blind Handy-man came stumbling back up the street, patting his hands against the wall of the group-home in order to feel his way forward. When Diamond saw him, she rushed outside and told one of the teen boys sitting in front of her building to go and help him. She gave him some money and instructed him to guide the Handy-man to wherever it was that he wanted to go and then to report back to her.

Back at the city center, a chaotic meeting would soon take place as those same city agents, some only seeing and some only hearing, returned and reported to Mr. Ruind (who was still the city controller at this time) and Mr. Screwtate, what they had either seen or heard. They could hardly give a complete picture as, the ones who saw the light, saw nothing else and could now only hear. And the ones who heard the voice, knew only that they heard a deafening voice but could not hear any of the words; now they could only see. Screwtate grew tired of trying to communicate with them and threw them all out of the office. "Seeing they don't see and hearing they don't hear," he mumbled under his breath.

"What?" Mr. Ruind asked him.

"Nothing, it's something my boss' ex-boss used to say."

"Wait. Your boss has a boss? I thought you said there was no one over your boss?"

"There isn't anymore. I said he's my boss' ex-boss. Mind the business I give you to mind, Ruind."

"You're talking about Newman and his father aren't you?"

Screwtate looked intently at Mr. Ruind, trying to decide if he should warn him to keep his mouth shut or rip his tongue out to ensure his silence. Mr. Ruind laughed, "What? You think I could become the city controller and not know the history of my city or the origin of the Chain Linked Nation? I know all about it.

But don't worry Screwtate. I've already chosen my side. Your secrets are safe with me."

This gave Screwtate some comfort. But he immediately began thinking of the next city controller and plotting what he could do to ensure perpetual confidentiality.

Meanwhile, the blind Handy-man and his aide were making their way to the west hills. The teen asked why it was that he wanted to go west; after all, it was said that the enemies of the city and the friends of Newman dwelt there. The Handy-man responded, "That may be. But right now, I'd rather be blind and fed in the hills than to see myself starving in the city."

"Aren't you the Handy-man who's going to bring the action of the V.I.P. room out onto the streets? I can't wait for that. I watch your shows on my connector. I know I'm not supposed to yet but it's so easy to get access, I just can't help myself."

The chain on the Handy-man's left hand got heavier as the teen spoke of these things.

"How close are we young man?

"We're right there. I can see the hills from here. Just a little while longer."

"If you point me in the right direction, is there anything between here and there that will cause me to stumble or fall."

"Yes. But not if you take your time and go straight ahead. You can't go one step to the left or to the right."

"Okay, then leave me here. Point me in the exact direction I need to go and leave me here."

The young man did as the Handy-man asked. He accurately aimed his elder and then stood back and watched him inch his way forward toward the foot of the hills.

It took him some time but the Handy-man eventually made it to his destination. When he began to fill the ground inclining beneath his feet, he stopped and called out, "Bro-man! Is Bro-man here? Newman sent me to talk to Bro-man! Is Bro-man here?" Bro-man came out from one of the caves near the bottom of the hill and said, "Newman sent you? Are you moving in? I'm so happy you're here. Thank you!"

"You knew I was coming?"

"Well . . . no. But now that you're here, I'm glad."

"You know who I am?"

"Nope. Doesn't matter."

"Then why are you so happy to see me?" the Handy-man asked.

"Well, if Newman sent you here, I take it that means you're moving in. The more crowded it gets down here, the more of a chance I have of moving up the hill. There's so much more work to be done when you're at the foot of the hills. So you just might be my ticket to move up. Wait, why are you looking over there, I'm right here."

"I can't see you. I can't see anything. Newman said that you would be able to fix me."

"Oh . . . I see. Sorry, no pun intended. Wait right here."

Bro-man went back into his cave and came back out with a menu. He opened it and held it out in front of the Handy-man and began reading and, every so often, asking him questions.

"Can you smell anything?"

"Yes, it smells like when Newman speaks, or when people speak about him to me."

"Okay. Then you're not far from sight. Have you ever read Newman's menu?"

"No."

"Give me your hand. Okay. Now fix your eyes on the place where I put your fingers. Alright, now read this."

As the Handy-man turned his head to where his fingers went, he began to see blurry images and very dim sights at the end of his hand. But the more he focused on the menu, the more his vision was restored and he could see what had been written there for his nourishment. Soon, his sight was fully restored. However, he noticed that he could not go on seeing for long without having to look again into the menu; for, the longer he looked away, the more his sight became like it was before he first peered into it.

Bro-man thought for a moment and then asked, "You said the aroma from the menu reminded you of when Newman spoke. How is it that you've heard him speak and yet you've never looked into a menu? Most people read the menu on their way up the hill. You have been to Newman's table, haven't you?" Bro-man looked down and saw that both of the stranger's hands were still bound, and extravagantly so.

The Handy-man responded, "I don't belong at Newman's table. I was on my way to put his friends on trial and then march them into Gehenna. But Newman himself confronted me with his light. He redirected my path and sent me here. He told me that you would instruct me on how I could lift his name, even with my heavy chains."

Then Bro-man understood the situation. "Ahhh. Now I see. He means to use your fancy chains for his honor."

"I want my chains, my skills, my whole life to adorn him. Tell me what I have to do to see him smile again."

"The N.I.N.T.E. has many initiatives going on in the city. A lot of us here have never been up to the top of the great hill, to Newman's table. We can only get on the hill with a city agent to escort us and that rarely leads to us getting pass the halfway point. But we always hope that Newman will 'meet us halfway', like the old saying goes. We've been waiting for somebody like you though."

"Somebody like me? What am I like?"

"Well, normally the city likes to send one agent up the hill with every citizen that requests to make the trip. But we know from experience that, if someone with shiny chains is requesting to go back up the hill, the city will try to pair that person up with someone with rusty chains who's been waiting to go. That way, they only have to send one agent to guard them both since, it's pretty safe to assume that the person with shiny chains is not trying to get to Newman; plus it saves the taxpayers money. Now, we have a bunch of our people waiting to put in requests to go up the hill. So, if we can get one of our people paired up with you and your flashy chains, our plan just might work."

"What plan?"

"Well, I was about to tell you. We've learned that, anytime someone with shiny chains shows up at the Chain Exchange gate, there's bound to be a delay. A long delay. It happens every time. The city agents have complained about it but there's nothing that can be done. So what we're thinking is this: we can take advantage of this situation. As long as our person with rusty chains gets paired with you, when you get to the gate all you have to do is let our guy go first; then you go second and the city agent last. This way, we can use the delay your chains will cause as an opportunity for one of our members to get away and start heading up the hill without the agent. And, if this works, we can keep running this initiative for a good little while. Then, eventually, your name will come up on the list and we'll find a way to sneak you pass the city agents too. You help us and we'll help you."

"What list?"

"We have a list of all our members whose right hands are still chained. And we plan to attempt to get everyone who wants to go, all the way up the hill at some point. But we have to be strategic. The city is very careful about who they let on the hill. So, are you in?"

"I'm game Bro-man. But, I'm thinking about your plan; why would the city believe that someone with shiny chains wants to go back up the hill? I already have what most people are seeking up there."

"Not necessarily. There are a lot of reasons why someone could want to go back. It could be that they fell in love with someone halfway up the hill. We know from reading the book of the N.I.N.T.E. that this is one of the ways the owner of that poisonous place tricks people and adds a third chain to the hearts of men and woman so that they can never be free from his influence.

The Handy-man laughed but Bro-man asked, "What's so funny?"

"Nothing, it's just that we call all of y'all, I mean, people we suspect of being Free-hands or N.I.N.T.E. members, 'third chains.' It's just a little funny to hear one of you use that term to refer to someone else."

"Well," Bro-man said, "when you think about it, that's what the owner of SOUL FOOLED is putting on people. Anyway, some people want to go back up the hill because they're seeing the lions and they believe there's refuge from them somewhere in the east hills. There are also people who go back because they are looking for freedom from their heavy chain and, some of those people have been told that their chain can be made lighter by the owner of SOUL FOOLED.

"The city still honors the old rule; a person can make as many trips up the hill as it takes to get where they've gotta go. So, as long as they don't catch on to what we're doing, we can run this initiative indefinitely. You just have to convince them that you have good reasons to keep coming back to the hill. Think you can do that?"

"If this is what will please Newman, then I have to do it. I used to think this was all . . . that you were all so crazy but now, nothing else makes sense except this. But wait, what happens if I end up on the hill and they've paired me up with another citizen of the city who's not a member of the N.I.N.T.E.?"

"Well, you just find a reason to reschedule. How soon would you be ready to make your first attempt?"

"I'm ready to do it now! Let's go. My only fear is, if I get caught, I'm going to miss the funeral of my young friend. And I owe it to her to be there?"

"Was she a Free-hand?"

"No."

"Do you have the hope?"

"What is 'the hope'?"

"That the Chain Exchange guard will come and claim her heavy chain . . . fight for it, if need be."

"No, I don't know anything about that."

Bro-man explained 'the hope' to him. This gave the Handy-man some encouragement but, not a great deal, for he did not know how close Treasure had come to being filled by Newman's food. No one did.

He spent the next couple of days learning the N.I.N.T.E.'s rules of engagement. They taught him the secret codes for communicating via connectors without raising suspicion. However, many who were there in the west hills did not trust him. When they heard that he was the one who put Straw-man on trial publically, they thought that he was there to spy on them and turn them in to the city.

But Bro-man embraced him and sought to convince them all that the Handy-man was a friend of

Newman and aware of the aroma. They were finally persuaded when the man they feared joined them for a meal, not just to consume it, but to concoct it; adding in what he had to offer which made the meal much more enjoyable. It was clear that, even though he had those shiny chains, which were now dull in his eyes, he had met with Newman and actually got to enjoy what many of them had yet to experience.

The Handy-man finally headed back to town to submit his request to travel up the great hill. When he got within city limits, his connector began to buzz with endless messages from Screwtate. He assumed that Screwtate wanted to know what happened to the arrests he planned to make but, he was wrong. He read the last message received: *Handy, where are you? I don't even care. Where are my food trucks? I gave you what you wanted now give me what I want. Half of the city is asking for the mobile meal/media center. Don't do this to me Handy-man. If you disappoint me, you'll regret it.*

The Handy-man sent a request to go 'head to head' with Screwtate and Screwtate accepted. They began their screen to screen chat, though they would no longer see eye to eye.

The Handy-man: *Send some agents to meet me at my Halfway's. I'll take them to the trucks. You'll just need to find drivers and people to monitor the cameras and broadcast what you want to see. But I can't do it. I need to go back up the hill.*

Screwtate: *For what?*

The Handy-man: *The other day, I'm sure you probably heard, something happened when I was on my way to arrest those people. But do you know what it was?*

Screwtate: *No. And I don't care.*

The Handy-man: *The city's enemy appeared to me.*

Screwtate: *Who?*

The Handy-man: *You know who. The name we can't communicate.*

Screwtate: *What did he say? What did he want?*

The Handy-man: *He showed me the lions. I've been running from them for days now. Some of my friends told me that I could find refuge from them if I went back up the hill. They say there's a bridge to the east. I've gotta go there. You do what you want with the trucks.*

Screwtate: *Suit yourself. You know the process for going up the hill. I'm not sending you so you'll need an* *agent to escort you like everyone else. Who's gonna run your Halfway's in the mean time?*

The Handy-man: *I don't care about that. I've gotta get rid of these lions.*

Screwtate laughed and told him: *I understand. Do what you've gotta do.*

The Handy-man was, of course, lying. But he was speaking Screwtate's language better than even Screwtate himself. He put in his request to go up the hill and received a response stating that an agent would be available within the next two days. He then sent word to Patchman. Patchman then connected with several N.I.N.T.E. members who were next on the list and had them put in requests as well. Unless there were already other requests from people in the city waiting to go up the hill, one of these N.I.N.T.E. members was certain to be paired up with the Handy-man.

That evening, he met the city agents sent from Screwtate at his establishment. He took them to the garage and showed them the food trucks and how to operate them. But he kept interrupting himself, pretending to be startled by the appearance of invisible lions. The agents laughed and made fun of him and, in the process, forgot to ask key questions about the operation of the trucks. Even though the Handy-man purposely neglected tell them everything they needed to know in order to work the equipment, he, nonetheless, still felt the chain on his left hand become heavier. He now regretted instructing them on how to feed and film the citizens of the city with the food from the V.I.P. room.

The next day, he got a message on his connector alerting him that the city agent responsible for escorting him was waiting to meet him at the food-court. It was now time. He had gone over it endlessly in his mind and was nervous about the entire plan. What if the city agent demanded to go through the gate first? What if there was no hold-up at the gate because of his shiny chains as Bro-man predicted there would be? What if the person selected to travel up the hill with him was not a member of the N.I.N.T.E.? Should he still embark on the journey? If Newman saw him again, would he be disappointed? All of this made the Handy-man a nervous wreck.

Just then, he got an instant thought from Diamond informing him that a friend of hers was going to be traveling up the hill with him. Diamond's friend was well aware of the plan, for he had been in touch with

Patchman. But Diamond did not know that the Handy-man was now looking to Newman. The last time she saw him, he was blind and unable to look anywhere at all. She thought that, whatever happened to him at the corner of her residence, had merely convinced him to make another trip up the hill to, perhaps, meet Newman. Diamond hoped that her friend might convince the Handy-man to look to Newman while they traveled the hill together. Her message simply read: *I just heard that my friend will be traveling up the hill with you today. I hope you both find what you're looking for up there, or should I say, what's up there looking for you both. I'll see you at Treasure's memorial service when you get back.*

Knowing that this particular aspect of the plan was secure encouraged him. He would not have to worry about being paired with someone who wasn't a N.I.N.T.E. member. He left home and headed up Straight Street to meet his escort and Diamond's friend. But when he reached the food-court, he saw a band of city agents and his nervousness returned. His chains rattled from all of his shaking as he stepped up and asked, "I'm supposed to be going up the hill today. Is one of you my escort?" His jittering actually helped his cause. One of the agents in the front turned and looked at the Handy-man. He then turned back around and shouted, "Ay! You got another one. And this guy looks like he's on the run from the lions." The agents all laughed as one of them stepped up from the back of the crowd.

The Handy-man's heart filled with fear as he looked up and saw Watchman coming toward him, looking as if he'd just finished an intense workout. His eyes pierced the Handy-man with a deadly serious stare. Perhaps this agent was still upset and out for revenge for the death of his friend Straw-man. "Just the man I been looking for," Watchman said. He forcefully grabbed the Handy-man's expensive chains with one hand. With his other hand, he motioned to summon the other traveler who had been waiting patiently for the Handy-man to arrive. The man got up and came over to introduce himself. "Hey. I'm Mr. Loverman."

The Handy-man introduced himself and then winked at his new travel partner. Mr. Loverman looked oddly at Watchman and did not wink back. Instead, he turned his head halfway around to gaze at the great hill with the most desperate look the Handy-man had ever seen.

"You two should get some food before we leave," Watchman suggested. But they both declined. Then he insisted, "Get some!" Neither of the travelers wanted to refuse him. But neither of them wanted to eat at Halfway's either. The Handy-man recalled that, the first time he went up the hill the agents encouraged him to eat from the food-court before his journey. He figured this might be some sort of test used to make sure that everyone going up the hill was still, at least, halfway content with being only halfway satisfied. "I'm tellin' you, I can't eat here," Mr. Loverman said. The Handy-man quietly cautioned him not to lose his cool. Then Watchman demanded, "Just get something. You can take it with you if you want. But get something!" And so they both did.

They left the food-court and began their journey. They had only been walking a little while when Mr. Loverman began unwrapping his food from Halfway's and nibbling on it. The Handy-man wondered to himself just what in the world Diamond's friend was doing. If he couldn't make it this far without resorting to eating that foul food, was he really ready to go all the way through with the plan? And what if he had a bad reaction to the effects of the food? He could jeopardize their whole mission.

Once they had gotten far enough that they could see the Chain Exchange gate, the Handy-man began looking around, searching for an escape route in case things went wrong. When Watchman noticed his nervousness, he began to slow down and pull the Handy-man's chains back in order to separate him from Mr. Loverman. After creating some distance between them, he stopped and said, "Alright, I think we're far enough now." But 'far enough' for what, the Handy-man wondered. It sounded like Watchman had come on the journey with a plan of his own; perhaps, a plan to do something about what happened to his friend Straw-man. And he had.

The Handy-man began backing away from the massive city agent. Watchman, for his part, began to smile and then advised him, "You can throw that food away. You're not going to need it anymore." He moved closer to the Handy-man.

"Wait a minute Watchman. What are you about to do? Back up. I'm not going to fight you."

"Put the food down."

"Look, I'm sorry for what happened to Straw-man. But that was a different me who did that. Please, whatever you're thinking . . ."

Watchman moved even closer to him, saying slowly, "Handy-man, put the food down."

Mr. Loverman was now quite a ways ahead of them. He was so determined to get where he was going that he did not even notice how much they were trailing behind. But when he heard the Handy-man pleading he turned halfway around to see just what was going on. Seeing the Handy-man's confrontational stance, Loverman threw his food on the ground and turned to watch the two of them. He felt like he was watching one of the Handy-man's productions from the V.I.P. room being lived out right in front of him.

Watchman finally got close enough and grabbed the Handy-man's wrists. He shook the food from Halfway's out of his hands. Towering over him, he grabbed the Handy-man by his shoulders and said, "I just wanted to thank you."

The Handy-man opened his eyes and looked up in disbelief, "You wanna what?"

"Thank you."

Getting ready to protect his face from a strike, the Handy-man asked, "Thank me, for what?"

Watchman informed, "For being willing to use your chains to help me lose mine. I know Newman will be pleased by your service to his people."

"Wait a minute," the Handy-man ordered—his heart still pounding in his chest, "what in the world are you talking about?"

But Watchman was just as confused. He asked, "Didn't my friend Diamond tell you that I'd be traveling up the hill with you today?"

The Handy-man looked up ahead to Mr. Loverman and shouted, "You're Diamond's friend right?"

"Whose friend?" Loverman shouted back.

"So wait," the Handed-man pleaded as he turned back to Watchman, "Why did you want us to get food from Halfway's before we left?"

"Well, we're going on a journey. None of us is supposed to be looking forward to eating at Newman's table. It would've looked suspicious if we left without eating from the food-court, don't you think?"

"Yes but," the Handy-man turned to Mr. Loverman and shouted, "You're part of the movement right?"

"What movement?" Loverman shouted impatiently, for he desperately wanted to get on with the journey.

The Handy-man shouted to him, "You refused the food from Halfway's at first; you don't eat there anymore right? You're looking forward to dining up on the hill aren't you?"

"Well, if you must know, like I told Watchman before you showed up. I can't eat anything really; I'm lovesick. The woman of my dreams is halfway up this hill and I've been dying to enter SOUL FOOLED to dine with her again. If it wasn't for Newman, I'd be up there with her right now. But he called himself 'rescuing me' from her the last time I was there. But not this time!"

Watchman finally understood the mix-up.

"Oh! You thought that Loverman was the one you were helping? No," he shook his head and laughed. Then he explained, "By the time you put your request in, this fellow was already scheduled to go up the hill today. So there was no way to get you and another member of the movement to travel together"

"Okay," the Handy-man accepted and then asked, "but how do you know about any of that? Where'd you come from with all this?"

"I'm sorry Handy. Let me explain. I heard about what happened to you when you were with those city agents and some of them came back blind. At first, I didn't know what to think. But then, I met Patchman and he told me everything."

"Wait, you heard what happened from who?"

"Well, I work with those agents you were with. Most of them are my friends. But they didn't really know what happened. So I began looking for you and Diamond told me you took a trip to the west hills. Then she put me in touch with Patchman. I didn't know about all the different N.I.N.T.E. initiatives until yesterday. I told Patchman my story and he told me what the N.I.N.T.E. was up to, how they intended to use your flashy chains. Then I checked and found out that you were scheduled to go up the hill with Loverman. I told Patchman and he confirmed that Loverman was not affiliated with the movement. So he and I decided to operate the same plan, just in reverse. Instead of using your chains to give someone else time to sneak off, we're gonna use your chains to buy me time to get ahead without Mr. Loverman knowing where I've gone off to. Then I can make it to the hilltop without him going back and saying anything to the city."

"So, you're not gonna kill me for what happened to Straw-man?"

Watchman laughed, then thought and said, "I'm more angry at myself for not being willing to risk my life for him, or for Newman. No. I wanted to come on this journey to tell you that . . ." he paused and then continued, "I forgive you for what happened to my friend. If Newman has forgiven you, how could I not?"

Watchman embraced the Handy-man and would not allow their chains to get in the way. The Handy-man acquiesced to the embrace but was still trying to put the pieces together in his mind, "So, that day, when I put Straw-man on trial and he asked you if you were a member of the N.I.N.T.E., you said 'no' but you really were?"

"No. I really wasn't. I meant it when I said 'not yet'. I was still trying to make up my mind about Newman."

"Oh. So, you were going to the meetings in the abandoned buildings? That's how you met Diamond? Did you ever meet my young friend Treasure?"

"No. I didn't go to any of the meetings in the buildings. I didn't meet any other members of the movement until Diamond put me on to Patchman yesterday. Straw-man had no contact with them when he was on house arrest. But I did see your young Treasure, once."

"Well, if you weren't a part of the movement when Straw-man died, how did you meet and become friends with Diamond?"

"Well, a little over a month ago, I was assigned to escort a citizen up the hill. A citizen named Mrs. Coalman. We met and instantly started becoming friends as I assisted her in ascending the hill. When we got just beyond the Chain Exchange gate, she called out to a young girl who was on her way down in quite a hurry. When the girl passed she told me that she was her Treasure. My mission was to take Mrs. Coalman halfway up, to SOUL FOOLED but, she kept telling me that she was going higher than that. She was funny; telling jokes about how she would overpower me and carry me to the top of the hill on her back if she had to."

The Handy-man laughed at the joke and, at the thought.

Watchman continued, "When we got halfway, the owner came out of SOUL FOOLED. I thought for sure that he would draw her in but, everything he said was meant to entice *me*. I forgot about Mrs. Coalman and started heading in to that old stale store. She begged me to come back and tried to pull me away. Then, those lions, which lay in wait there, all of a sudden disobeyed the owner . . . or maybe they obeyed him; I don't know. But they attacked me. And they almost made me their meat.

"But, the next thing I knew, I was being carried away from there. I was in complete shock, at first. I'm thinking, 'Man! She wasn't joking! This little old woman is actually carrying me on her back!' Only to find out that it was Newman who had rescued me. He set me down back on the road and invited me to travel up the hill with him and Mrs. Coalman. But I didn't trust him. I told him, 'thanks, but no thanks.' I told Mrs. Coalman that I would wait for her halfway down the hill, where it was safe. I stayed down there starving. I wasn't about to come back into the city without the citizen that I was supposed to be guarding. I was tempted to go across that bridge to the east. But then, finally, almost a whole three days later, Mrs. Coalman came back down saying she had a new name.

"She talked about the restaurant and Newman. I wanted to believe her but, I just couldn't. I told her that, when we got back into the city, I would help her hide her free hand to get pass the agents. But, after that, I told her that we could only remain friends if she never mentioned Newman to me again. I was not about to risk my job or my life for her. She agreed but, you know her. She has a way of cooking up something for Newman without you even knowing it until the meal is almost ready. And by then, you're hooked.

"But I still wasn't convinced. So, on the night that Straw-man was arrested, I signed up to go guard the jail. My plan was to prove Newman or his followers to be about treason. I unlocked Straw-man's jail cell while he was asleep and left it wide open. I was about to wake him up and pretend that I was asleep, just to see what he would do. But then, all of a sudden, the whole jail shook and everyone's door flew open. All the prisoners wanted to escape but instead of joining them, Straw-man convinced them not to. And he did that for the sake of me and my family, since he knew that Mr. Ruind would have surely punished my family for my failure. That's when I began to believe that

Newman Is Not The Enemy. I put Straw-man on house arrest so that I could question him about Newman without anyone else knowing."

The Handy-man affirmed him with, "That's so similar to my story." Then he asked, "So, what sealed it for you Watchman? What made you fully look to Newman?"

"Well, when that mob took Straw-man down to Gehenna, I followed them and I watched. I was ashamed that I did not stop them. I felt that Newman wanted me to and yet, I did nothing. I kept saying to myself, 'but what if Newman is wrong?' Well, right before they threw Straw-man into the flames, I spoke to Newman in my heart and asked him to do something about it; like the stories I had heard. But then, when nothing happened in the fires, something happened in me. I remember saying to Newman, 'Even if you don't do anything, I'll still look to you.' The fact that Straw-man was willing to die for Newman made me want to live for him."

The Handy-man asked, "So, did anything happen in the fire? Anything at all?"

"Yes. But I don't know what. After they threw Straw-man in, it was like they had thrown something combustible in there because, all of a sudden, flames started shooting everywhere and people began running from Gehenna. They ran pass me and I was just trying to shield my body from the crowd. But once or twice, when I looked back into the fires, I think I saw... I think I saw what I was hoping to see."

Watchman and the Handy-man walked slowly as they talked and shared their experiences with one another. Finally, they reached the Chain Exchange gate and the tall guard who stood there informed them, "No chains on the hill beyond this point." By now, Mr. Loverman had gone through the gate and was already a good ways ahead of them. So they needed not to proceed with any chicanery. Watchman went through and was given the time he would need to make it to the top and back. Then the guard turned to the Handy-man and said, "I'm sorry, I don't have the key to your chains. I'm not going to go back and forth with you about it. If you want, I can try all the keys I have here or call someone from the top of the hill and we can wait for them to arrive, but they're just going to tell you the same thing."

The Handy-man informed him, "No, that's cool. I wasn't really planning on making the trip this time anyway. But, what if I wanted to? How do I get rid of these chains in order to travel up?"

The guard replied, "You can't. You'd have to travel with those chains and almost no one ever makes that trip successfully."

"But would you let me try?" the Handy-man pled.

"You came this way before didn't you? You know that the road ahead is steep and very challenging to unchained travelers, let alone someone with your weighty entanglements. In fact, from what I've seen, it'd be easier for you to fit your body through one of the links in your chain than for you to make it up this hill wearing those flashy fetters."

"Will you let him try? Or are you saying it is impossible?" Watchman asked.

"It is impossible, for him. But with Newman, even the impossible becomes possible. But I do not know how."

The Handy-man asked, "You've been doing this forever. I'm sure you can look at these chains of mine and tell me how long it should take me to reach the top can't you?"

"I could take an educated guess, sure."

"Okay, how long do you think?"

The Chain Exchange guard looked at his chains closely and supposed, "About four days just to make it halfway. And by then, you'd be so weak that you would almost certainly give in to the very first temptation thrown your way at SOUL FOOLED."

The Handy-man smiled sorrowfully and said, "I wish I would've made this journey for real years ago. But I think Newman knew what he was doing. He didn't even try to stop me the first time I came this way. But, you know what? Bro-man was wrong. The old cliché is wrong. Newman doesn't just meet us halfway. He came to me, all the way down in the city when I wasn't even looking for him. In fact, I was seeking to put him into Gehenna bit by bit. But I saw him wearing my heavy chain and I know I'll be at his table one day!"

He turned to Watchman and encouraged him, "You go ahead. I have a funeral to attend in two days. And sir," he said as he turned to the Chain Exchange guard, "I hear you've been known to shake those services up a bit when you want to. I hope you're planning to come and cause a scene."

He smiled and then turned back to head toward the city. But Watchman called out to him and said, "Take this, I think it's more for where you'll be then where I'm going." He gave the Handy-man his menu and then, let him go on his way.

Once back in the city, the Handy-man traveled back down Straight Street to where he had parked his truck and then headed home. As he drove along, he passed one of his cruel creations; the mobile meal/media center. There he saw the citizens of Nameless City enjoying the deadly delights of the V.I.P. room, right on the street. He received comfort, only, from noticing that his chains did not get any heavier as he passed them by; for he did not take any part nor take any pleasure in what he saw. He went home and barricaded himself inside. There he did nothing, except read his menu, while he waited to attend the young Treasure's funeral.

EPISODE ELEVEN
A Beautiful Noise

In two days' time, the final preparations had been made. It was now time for the service where friends and family would get to say goodbye to Treasure. At ten o'clock on the dot, things got underway in the emotionally partitioned parlor where her physical frame was placed on display. The room was filled, halfway with sadness and grief and on the other side, with mostly hope and anticipation.

This division was mainly because, on one side sat family members, along with friends from school and co-workers from Halfway's. But on the other side, there sat Her-man and the young Khalil, and behind them, the Handy-man along with several N.I.N.T.E. members who came to support Diamond and join her in 'the hope.' More members from the movement would have joined her, but there were other funerals to attend that day since, Treasure did not die alone.

The service began with a song sung by one of Treasure's cousins. It was a bit off-putting (not the song, for the songstress had a lovely voice). There was disturbing commotion that could be heard coming from another room in the same building, right in the middle of her melody. A few of Treasure's family members complained to the funeral director about the disturbance, asking "What's that noise?" But, the N.I.N.T.E. members in the room smiled and responded, "Isn't it a beautiful noise?"

Then, the officiating city minister over family affairs asked if anyone had anything they wished to say. A few people lined up to speak their last words to Treasure. Finally, just before the open mic was closed, the Handy-man got up to say his piece. He was greeted with piercing stares from members of Treasure's family who blamed him for the time she spent working behind the dark, red door.

As he stood there, wondering what they must all be thinking, he struggled to put his own thoughts and feelings into words. In the silence, loud cheers could be heard coming from elsewhere in the building. One would imagine that someone was having a raucous home-remodeling party, for it sounded as if heavy furniture was being moved around amid loud shouts and yells. The Handy-man turned and looked back at Treasure laying peacefully in her body's last bed. When it was quiet again, he began.

"Treasure was searching for something. I don't... I didn't know what she was looking for until just a few days ago. So how was I going to help her find it, you know? I want to be able to say I tried but, I didn't. I tried to help her while helping myself first. That never helps anybody but yourself. We've got to learn to put others first, you know? I know that now. I promise, from this point on, I'm going to be, like a *new man*. I'm always going to put someone else first. Some of you in here know who I'm talking about." He looked to his left as he said these words. He then paused and pulled out an electronic device to place in the casket with Treasure.

"This... this coloring nook belonged to her. I got it for her when she was just a little girl. She loved this thing. But you know what? It's funny because, I've been doing some reading lately and, I've learned that this coloring nook is actually a great example of something that I hope Treasure finally realized. It's kind of like . . . you know how each individual screen can hold an image . . . I mean, we are all like a . . . see, there's a father who . . ."

He struggled to express his thought. He saw what he wanted to say clearly in his mind but, how to say it in a way that communicated the actual truth of things without confusing anyone? He wanted to speak about Newman and his father but could not figure out a way to do it hypothetically, in accordance with the N.I.N.T.E.'s rules of engagement.

He was about to say what he meant plainly and risk revealing his affiliation with the movement and his affection for Newman. But, just then, the doors swung open and two tall figures, dressed in black, seemed to float through the doorway and progress down the center aisle of the room. Each held several chains in his hand, having collected them from other memorial services which had taken place that same evening. The Handy-man saw them coming toward him and quickly moved out of the way and headed back to his seat.

Once they made it to the front, the two figures stood, side by side, looking into the casket. "Let the record show that the deceased still has both of her chains connected to her wrists," one of them announced. "I concur," the other responded. "I will now unlock the chain connected to the right hand," the one on the right said. Those in attendance who had been up the great hill began to whisper that the one on the right was the Chain Exchange guard. The other one, they rightly presumed, was from the Chain Linked Nation.

The Chain Exchange guard leaned in to unlock the chain with his large skeleton key, while the representative from the Nation began to ball his left hand up until it became a tightly packed fist. Once the chain was unlocked, the guard put his key away and stood with his right hand resting on the top of the casket. The representative from the Nation began to slowly reach his right hand in to retrieve the chain while he watched carefully to see if and when guard's right hand moved at all.

The crowd watched, some simply waiting for the one on the left to take the chain, expecting nothing more. But the members of the N.I.N.T.E. movement sat on the edges of their seat, knowing what could possibly come next and hoping to actually see such an occurrence. The chain-linked representative finally managed to get his hand all the way in and loosely wrapped his fingers around Treasure's heavy chain. But now, he must manage to pull it out.

He began to retract his right arm, even as he lifted his left hand to prepare to strike his austere associate. By now, he was shaking so badly that Treasure's heavy chain could be heard rattling all the way in the back of the room. And not only her chain, but the scared chain snatcher was, himself, restrained with many heavy chains which were now making their own messy music for all to hear. In his nervousness, he dropped Treasure's chain and it fell back down onto the body she once wore. At that moment, the Chain Exchange guard got tired of waiting and plunged his right hand into the casket to firmly grip Treasure's heavy chain.

The representative from the Chain Linked Nation summoned his left hand and sent it surging towards the head of the Chain Exchange guard. But the guard caught his fist with his only free hand, since his other hand still held Treasure's chain. The Handy-man, Diamond and the other N.I.N.T.E. members in the crowd began to cheer wildly. However, the Chain Exchange guard silenced them all when he took Treasure's chain in his fist and sunk it into the chest of the representative from the Nation. "Here!" he said, his voice firm and full of finality. "Take it!"

The representative stumbled backwards and grabbed hold of Treasure's chain while he tried to pretend that he was not also rubbing his chest to soothe it from the blow. He took off running back up the center aisle an exited the building. Those who cheered now began weeping, for they knew there was no more hope for their young friend. The guard from the gate glared at the guests in the room, his eyes warning them not to come to the same fate as the young Treasure. Then, without saying a word, he left.

Most of the attendees at the funeral applauded the fact that the ceremony did not end in violence. They were also relieved that Treasure's chain went to the representative from the Chain Linked Nation. "That's where the chains came from and that's where they should return," was a popular saying in the city. This is what most people were used to and they did not know how to want anything different.

The Handy-man, however, motioned for Diamond to follow him as he went after the Chain Exchange guard. They, along with a few other members of the N.I.N.T.E. movement, caught up to him and asked why he did not fight for Treasure's heavy chain. Didn't she look to Newman, they implied.

But the guard informed them, "It is true that Treasure eagerly sought to hear the comforting words of Straw-man and others but, she only came near in order that she might be far from the lions, for she saw them much less when in the company of the N.I.N.T.E. However, while she enjoyed and desired refuge from those beasts, she did not desire fellowship with Newman for she only looked to him halfway. Nor did she desire freedom from her heavy chain. It is impossible to dine at SOUL FOOLED or Halfway's and then come to Newman's table for dessert. Her taste buds have been ruined and she would not be pleased by what Newman would serve. She has enjoyed her meal in the Nameless City and, for dessert, has reserved a place in Gehenna."

Both Diamond and the Handy-man thought about their own foul appetites before they met Newman. They, too, had ruined their taste buds and thought his food repulsive. This drew their attention to how merciful Newman had been in allowing their appetite for true soul's food to be restored from nothing at all, for they should have been worse off than Treasure.

The Chain Exchange guard turned to the Handy-man and said, "When I first met you, you thought you had a fix for everything and everyone. Now that Newman has lightened your load and will ultimately free and strengthen your hand, I hope you will allow him to do the fixing through you, in the ways he sees fit, and not according to your own wisdom." The Handy-man nodded his head and with that, the guard left them.

As they traveled back to Diamond's group-home apartment, the Handy-man tried to comfort her but, how much comfort could there be? He apologized for the role he played in Treasure's story and for not playing a better one. And she forgave him, mainly because Newman had already forgiven him; how, then, could she not?

Down at the city center, Mr. Screwtate was meeting with Mr. Ruind. His concerns about the next city controller had begun to bother him and he was planning to do something about it.

"Ruind, tell me, have you told your son about me; about my nation's history and the history of this city?"

"Yes. But he's been hanging around your wife's son, Her-man. So he's got two sides to the same story and not a very flattering picture of you."

"I can see the way he looks at me. I don't like it. I think I like your grandson better to replace you as controller."

"Replace me? You planning on getting rid of me?"

"No. Of course not." But Screwtate really was planning to do so. "I'm just thinking . . . no one lives forever."

"I know no one lives forever. But how do you know that I'll die before you Screwtate? We're probably about the same age."

This comment showed Screwtate that Ruind did not even halfway know what he thought he knew about the Chain Linked Nation. So he played along.

"Right. I might die first Ruind. But I'm just saying, if you should happen to die first, and before our deal goes through, I want someone to take your place who doesn't already have a negative view of me. Your grandson is young and untainted. He's ripe to be groomed for the job."

"Do me a favor Screwtate, keep your thoughts off my grandson. And your hands even further off. If he wants to go into politics then he will, and if not, I won't force him. Your best bet is to warm up to my son because he will be the next controller unless the city votes him out."

But Screwtate was already working on a scheme to discredit Ivan Ben Ruind the 2nd in order to make room for the 3rd. However, he was not the only one with plans for the next leader of the city. The N.I.N.T.E. was focusing on Ruind number two and saw him as the key factor in several of their new initiatives. But those adventures, along with all the exploits of Watchman, are stories for another occasion.

The Handy-man, now with his unchained heart, served as much as he could, as long as Newman gave him the strength to lift his hands. He eventually went to live in the west hills and insisted that he be permanently placed at the bottom of the hill, where there was always work to be done. This allowed Bro-man to move up just a little higher on the hill and the two of them became great friends.

Bro-man, who got his new name in the hills by always talking about his connection to one of the movement's first leaders, was always quick to show off his digital picture to everyone in order to prove that Trumaine was his brother. And as often as he did, the Handy-man would tell him about Her-man and young Khalil back in the city and how much they looked like Trumaine. Bro-man did not believe him then but, one day, he would get to see for his self.

The Handy-man never went up the north hill, to Newman's table. He was content that his Hilltop Hero had come down to see him in the city. He would wear his heavy chain until Newman returned to the city or, until the Chain Exchange guard came to his funeral to unlock it and, hopefully, more than that; to fight for it and reclaim it. And of course, Newman did return to the city before then.

But even as he finally sat with Newman, rather, with E-man, around the unending table in Emmanuel City, the Handy-man was keenly aware of just how much he did not deserve to be there. And while others longed to look into the light that located Emmanuel's presence in order to see his face, the Handy-man would not look very long. For he remembered the smile he once saw and was still unsure whether, when he looked at Emmanuel's face, he would see that smile again or, might he see the look of displeasure that he also saw when Newman's light first confronted him?

But, there was one thing that he knew for sure: in the newly built city his hands were now totally free and he was now able to serve Emmanuel without any restraints whatsoever. Back when the city was nameless, before Newman returned, the Handy-man tried so hard and for so long to lift his hands in order to serve and help and undo the harm all his 'fixes' had caused. Yet, try as he may, he could only do so much. But now, in Emmanuel City, without those chains to hold them down, his hands could finally fully extend into the air and they always seemed to be rising higher, like a perpetual, preemptive strike against inertia. And, after hearing this tale, who could blame him?

Epilogue:
Arrival of the Watchers

When E-man had told about this much of the Handy-man's story, he saw that the hearts of the other guests around his table had softened toward that diligent servant. They were ashamed that they suspected foul play or favoritism. But one of them asked Emmanuel, "Doesn't the Handy-man know that he can never earn your smile or repay your kindness? Doesn't he know that his good now can never outweigh his bad from before? And that it is *your* good, not his own, that secures his place at this table? If so, why does he work so much?"

Emmanuel replied, "It is not so much guilt as it is gratitude. He is doing now what he wishes he could have done before his hands became so heavy. Though he will soon realize that he can never do enough to fully express his gratitude, and he will finally sit and stare and see my face. Then he will know that I have been smiling on him this entire time. But he will also learn that my smile is only a reflection of my father's, and that my father has been smiling toward him since before he was born; before he could even do anything good or bad. This is how it is with all those who find their place around this table. And if you think the Handy-man works a lot now . . . just wait until you see how he serves after he comes to understand these things."

When Emmanuel had thus spoke, the sky began lighting up as what appeared to be bright, shining stars shot across the upper atmosphere and fell to the west of the city, where there was a far-reaching, breathtaking crystal sea. Many of the guests were frightened and many others wanted to go and investigate. They looked to Emmanuel in order to follow his lead but, he did not move or even

Epilogue: Arrival of the Watchers

acknowledge the odd occurrence. "What is that?" they asked. "That," E-man replied, "is the answer to your earlier question. Go and see."

A large number of his guests then arose and went to track the streaks of fire that had been left in the sky by the falling stars. When they found what they followed, they were all stunned and amazed. Some cheered and others cried tears of joy. Now, I could tell you what they found. And, believe me, I would thoroughly enjoy doing so. But, that is a story for another time. For this, what you have just read, was merely the astounding story of a broken Handy-man and the Handy-man's fix.

It is possible to be a father and not be a good father-figure. It is also possible to be a good father-figure and not actually be a father. Because we have so many of the former, we now need many more of the latter.

–The Author

Made in the USA
Coppell, TX
25 August 2022